"Candyce is the rea lots of unfounded ideas and growing complexity, Candyce shows us that simplicity, love and power are always God's best. You will find this book a refreshing and interesting journey into a world where only those, like Candyce, who know their God, thrive and cause others to do so too. Jump in!"

Andy Reese, author of *Freedom Tools for Overcoming Life's Tough Problems*

"Candyce Roberts is the most gifted person I know in regard to helping traumatized people regain the life that was stolen from them in their youth. This book is filled with insights and practical advice tested and proven by years of experience in the healing ministry. It has given me more confidence to pray for the severely wounded."

Dr. Jack Deere, author and pastor

"I heartily recommend this book to you if you are in any way ministering to or praying for those who have been significantly traumatized, and especially for those of you who love them and need to understand them better. Dr. Roberts's considerable experience has here been presented in a very commonsense, straightforward, readily digestible manner that is easily employed. It will provide you with a solid understanding to meld with your existing ministry foundations that will allow you to broaden your ability to effectively minister to the brokenhearted."

Jim Banks, founder/director,
House of Healing Ministries,
Asheville, North Carolina / Campbellsville, Kentucky

"Dr. Candyce Roberts writes, teaches and ministers with undeniable clarity. Few understand the depth of the trauma that she writes about. This topic is often denied, misunderstood or seen as unresolvable. This book is not just educational; it provides hope for any whose lives have been impacted by such tragedy."

Stephen Johnson, Stephen Johnson & Associates
Counseling Center, Lexington, Kentucky

"The most informative book I've read on inner healing. Her simple yet profound examples explain how to help the most traumatized people, yet the principles apply to us all. Candyce has helped countless people in our church and trained up our prayer team. Her book will be a welcome addition!"

Chuck Snekvik, associate pastor,
Greater Boston Vineyard Church

HELP
FOR THE
FRACTURED
SOUL

HELP

FOR THE

FRACTURED
SOUL

Experiencing Healing and Deliverance
from Deep Trauma

Candyce Roberts

Chosen
a division of Baker Publishing Group
Minneapolis, Minnesota

© 2012 by Candyce Roberts

Published by Chosen Books
11400 Hampshire Avenue South
Bloomington, Minnesota 55438
www.chosenbooks.com

Chosen Books is a division of
Baker Publishing Group, Grand Rapids, Michigan

Printed in the United States of America

Library of Congress Cataloging-in-Publication Data
Roberts, Candyce.
    Help for the fractured soul : experiencing healing and deliverance from deep trauma /Candyce Roberts ; foreword by Neil T. Anderson.
        p.   cm.
    ISBN 978-0-8007-9532-0 (pbk. : alk. paper)
    1. Spiritual healing. 2. Prayer—Christianity. I. Title.
BL65.M4R63 2012
259'.42—dc23   2012001936

Unless otherwise identified, Scripture quotations are from the New American Standard Bible®, copyright © 1960, 1962, 1963, 1968, 1971, 1972, 1973, 1975, 1977, 1995 by The Lockman Foundation. Used by permission.

Scripture quotations identified NIV are from the Holy Bible, New International Version®. NIV®. Copyright © 1973, 1978, 1984, 2011 by Biblica, Inc.™ Used by permission of Zondervan. All rights reserved worldwide. www.zondervan.com

Cover design by Dan Pitts

12   13   14   15   16   17   18   7   6   5   4   3   2   1

This book is dedicated to my favorite person, my husband and best friend, Ray.

You have encouraged me in the direction of my destiny for 33 years. You have taught me the value of heritage and sowing into the lives of those who can benefit from what the Father has blessed in us. I am grateful to you for calling forth what you saw in me long before my awareness. This book is a result of your encouragement. Thank you, Ray.

Contents

Foreword

For years I have been traveling around the United States equipping the Church to establish her people alive and free in Christ. I encountered a number of pastors and counselors who were trying to help victims of satanic ritual abuse (SRA). I first I thought it was an anomaly. This couldn't possibly be widespread. Could it?

I come from a very conservative background, and the idea that people actually worship Satan was not part of my experiential and educational grid. I could not even fathom why anyone would want to do that. But it is happening all over America, and their rituals contain abuses that defy the imagination. So horrible are the atrocities that the vast majority of victims dissociate in order to survive. For most victims, a relatively "normal" person presents him- or herself to the world, which some call the host personality, but these individuals are plagued by dissociated parts or other personalities. Each personality represents a portion of time in the person's past, and each has a story to tell.

Their diagnosis is dissociative identity disorder (DID), and treatment varies from one discipline to another. I have heard secular counselors admit that the Church should somehow be involved—even though they don't believe the message. Their track record is abysmal, because you cannot resolve this problem without taking into account the reality of the spiritual world, and there is no wholeness without Christ. Even Christian counselors have little success unless they understand the spiritual battle for the mind.

All SRA survivors hear voices in their heads. Some are condemning, accusing and blasphemous. Others sound like human personalities, of which many are children. Those "voices" could be demonic, or they could be fragmented personalities. The pastoral error is to assume they are all demonic and try to get rid of them through various deliverance techniques. But what if some of those voices are personalities? You cannot get rid of them, because they are part of the person. The counselor's error is to believe that the voices are all fragmented personalities and try to integrate them into the host personality. But what if they are demons? The survivor usually can tell one from the other.

I have helped thousands who have no dissociated parts find their freedom from deceiving spirits. But I have never seen an SRA victim who has a true DID without also having a demonic problem. It is possible, but I have not yet seen it, and neither have most of the Christian counselors and pastors that I know. Working with these dear people requires a lot of patience and discernment.

Another troubling observation is the varied explanations for the origin of the problem. Every year I would hear a new theory. I started to wonder what is wrong with this picture. For years I have said that the right prescription does not yet exist, but when it does it will likely be something like what Dr. Candyce Roberts offers. Dr. Roberts has not succumbed to all the pat answers and quick fixes that so plague the industry. She has gotten away from counseling techniques borrowed from the secular world and learned to depend on the Wonderful Counselor who leads us into all truth and sets us free. She also has the right goal, which is not integration. A fractured mind is the problem, but integration is not an end. It is a beginning. The same reasoning holds for getting people free in Christ, which also is not an end, but a beginning. These people have a dysfunctional background and have never learned how to live the "normal" Christian life in a community of grace.

This book does not supply all the answers. No one book can, but it will make a valuable contribution to those who are struggling to get free and to those who are helping them. Dr. Roberts does not cover the demonic interference, and when I questioned her about it, she simply said, "I do the same thing you do." So you may want to read *The Bondage Breaker* (Anderson, Harvest House) as a companion to this book if this is all new to you. In Dr. Roberts's book, you will find a seasoned and sensitive journey to wholeness and inner healing.

Dr. Neil T. Anderson
Founder and President Emeritus
of Freedom in Christ Ministries

Acknowledgments

To my daughters, I am blessed by whom you have become in the Lord. You represent Him well. Your wise choices have resulted in godly husbands who in turn have become godly fathers and leaders in the Kingdom, partnering with you in establishing households that seek His face. I am thankful that you demonstrate the things of God that we prayed over you when you were born. Thank you for staying on the path.

Heather, Summer, Kendal—I love you just because you're you!

To Dr. Ed Smith. Thanks, Ed, for including me in the early journey of TPM, through which I fell in love with the transforming power of the Holy Spirit.

To Dr. Neil T. Anderson—you have provided the Kingdom with such a valuable teaching tool with truth regarding who we are in Christ. I am grateful.

To my parents—thanks for always telling me that I could do whatever I was determined to do.

To Jack Deere—thank you for becoming my writing mentor and sharing your knowledge and time with me. Your devotion to this book has been a true blessing. I appreciate you as a teacher and a dear friend.

1

Helping the Hurting

Bob came to me for prayer ministry because of the many conversations going on in his head. On this particular afternoon he sat in my office on the couch across from me, his plain shirt buttoned tightly around his neck. His pants, which were many sizes too large, were cinched tightly around his waist with a belt. Bob's clothing seemed to match his personality: He was uptight.

Bob told me how the voices in his mind argued nonstop. They came from people of different ages and both sexes. His eyes filled with shame as he admitted that he often dressed like a woman because some of the personalities inside him believed that they were female. He said he felt as if evil spirits were tormenting him because the confusion of the voices was disrupting his daily life. One day, the females and males were arguing over his true gender. In the confusion and clamor, he realized that he could not figure out the truth about who he was.

Suddenly, his demeanor changed, and I was no longer talking with Bob; I was talking with one of the female child personalities who lived within his mind. The man who was Bob curled up in the corner of my couch and pulled a blanket over his head. He began to cry and spoke in a child's small voice. "God can't love me," said the little girl inside. "He can't love me because He allowed those big people to do bad things to me."

As I talked with the little girl, I learned information that Bob as an adult had not been aware of. I asked the little girl what had happened to her, and she said that big people had beat and raped her, and that they were dressed like Jesus. In her child's mind, there was no distinction between truth and the deception. "Jesus hurt me," she said.

Further, these men who were dressed like Jesus had told young Bob over and over that God could never love him. Suffering from the torture, his mind had developed a separate personality to deal with and then hold this trauma. In other words, because of the occult abuse, Bob's mind had fractured into different personalities. On that particular day of torture, this little girl had come forward and stored away the memory with its pain.

I had seen a change of personalities in Bob many times before. He remembered much of the abuse that the satanic cult had done to him, but this was the first time a little girl personality had emerged. He had heard her voice for a long time, and voices of other little girls, but he had not been able to admit this—even to himself.

Now the child's voice spoke from under the blanket once more. "God doesn't love dirty little boys." Then the little girl stopped talking.

The day, many years before, when Bob's tormented soul had believed the lie that God could never love him, the cult had succeeded in its chief goal. Now that the lie was uncovered, it was our job to reveal the truth.

Where It Begins

This book is birthed out of a fifteen-year journey of helping those who have been highly traumatized find healing. I am referring to individuals who have survived some combination of severe emotional, physical, mental, sexual, spiritual or occult abuse. Abuse often damages minds and emotions to such a degree that the sufferers live in despair. They frequently cause the people trying to help them to despair as well. I want to share my victories, challenges and failures in my attempt to help the traumatized find healing in Jesus Christ, who said that He came to set the captives free (see Luke 4:18).

I define the *highly traumatized* as those who have survived long-term intentional abuse that began in childhood and often continued into adulthood. This abuse was perpetrated by family members, authority figures or caregivers. These perpetrators continually intimidated, manipulated and, when deemed necessary, used violence to secure the submission of their victims.

The abuse these individuals suffered is not limited to the physical, mental and emotional. I use the term *spiritual abuse* to include the perpetrators' manipulation of Scripture and biblical principles, as well as distortion of the character of our heavenly Father, Jesus and the Holy Spirit, to secure the silence of their victims. One abuser told his daughter, "If this was wrong, God would have stopped it." Another told his daughter, "God said you are supposed to honor your parents. If you tell anyone about this, you are betraying me, and God will punish you."

Occult abuse is trauma given at the hands of a cultic group, such as Satanists, and it always contains intentional spiritual abuse. Occult abuse is often referred to as *ritual abuse* because satanic worshipers follow various ceremonial patterns in traumatizing their victims. They use systematic sexual, physical, emotional, mental and spiritual abuse to fragment their victims' minds.

This type of abuse usually takes place initially in an occult environment where the occult members dress like Jesus, the child's parents or other significant people in the child's life in order to confuse him or her about who is safe and who is unsafe. They want to blur as many lines in the child's life as possible. The occult members understand that when young children experience extreme terror and confusion their minds will fracture. The occultists can then begin to lie to the fragmented child personality and create a way to control the child for many years.

Once the occult members gain control of fragmented child personalities, they can reinforce the child's fear in less traumatic ways. They can, for example, meet the child in the hall of his elementary school, address a specific child personality by name and remind that personality that they will hurt the people he loves if he tells what happened to him.

Individuals who come out of situations of extensive abuse—occult, incestuous or otherwise—are known as *survivors*. Individuals who come out of occult abuse are often referred to as *satanic ritual abuse*, or SRA, *survivors*. The result of most abuse is that victims become confused about our heavenly Father, Jesus, the Holy Spirit and scriptural truths. They are confused about who they are and what they mean to God.

Roadblocks to Help

Survivors face many challenges in getting help. Many who remember instances of abuse suffer shame and find them hard to talk about. They also are afraid that no one will believe them. This is particularly true regarding occult abuse.

I have found in the Body of Christ two rather large schools of thought regarding occult abuse that hinder these survivors from getting help. The first is composed of Christians who do not believe that occult abuse really occurs. They question, for instance, the validity of trauma memories, which, often, are the only evidence available that these horrors have taken place.

The severity of occult abuse is beyond the comfort zone of many believers, keeping them from acknowledging this present evil. There are many fears and many lies entangled with embracing the reality of the intentional evil involved in ritual abuse. I am concerned that the focus within the Body of Christ has been narrowed to debate and not to freedom for those who have been systematically abused in this manner.

Occult abuse is not a new phenomenon; it is referred to in the Old Testament as an evil practice that polluted the land through blood shed for evil sacrifices (see Leviticus

18:21; Deuteronomy 9:4; 12:31; 18:9–12; 2 Kings 16:3; 17:15; Psalm 106:38; Jeremiah 19:4–5; 32:35). The gods that are worshiped often change, but the evil practices remain the same. The web of occult abuse has left many brokenhearted people trapped in darkness. It is my desire to encourage prayer warriors and prayer ministers to expand our vision of setting the captives free to include those who have suffered at the hands of occultists.

The other school of thought in the Body of Christ includes those who accept the validity of occult abuse but feel unqualified to deal with those who have been hurt by it. Take, for instance, one common scar of the highly traumatized: a divided or fragmented mind. Medically, this is labeled *dissociative identity disorder* or DID. This scar poses a threat to many prayer ministers. They feel that they are not qualified to address such an extreme disorder.

Please hear this: It is critically important that we operate only within our scope of qualification when we minister God's love to others. If we are not medical doctors or qualified counselors, we should never diagnose a person's condition. If we are not licensed to comment on a person's medication, we should not comment. We should not make promises of any fashion during times of inner healing prayer ministry.

As Christian believers, however, we are precisely qualified to lead anyone into the presence of our heavenly Father, where healing for the most dramatic physical, mental, emotional and spiritual issues can take place. Survivors of any kind of abuse should not be excluded from the hope and promise of His love. The severity of a person's condition will not intimidate prayer ministers who are confident of their spiritual role when they pray for the traumatized. We speak truth to lies about biblical principles and the character of our Father. We set the captive survivors of abuse free by leading them into the healing presence of Jesus.

The Issue of Trust

It is, of course, a condition of this healing journey that the survivors themselves must want help. Most survivors are hampered by issues of trust. This can make for a frustrating cycle: Abuse survivors often report an inability to live life in an emotionally healthy manner, yet they often do not trust anyone who attempts to help them. They are angry and confused because they have been deceived, manipulated and controlled by those in positions of authority.

This is not surprising when you realize that abusers often present themselves as Christians who love and serve God. Still, it complicates the healing process, not only because it makes the victims distrust their heavenly Father, but it can also make them distrust their own feelings. I have heard women say, "Well, my father loved God. What he did was not so bad."

Helping abuse survivors understand the power of personal choice is crucial. Abuse survivors do not believe that they have choices because they have lived in powerlessness for years. They had no choice to stop the abuse; how can they stop the pain now? Pain and shame have simply become facts of daily existence. It is essential that abuse victims know that God will not force Himself on them. He will not violate them like their abusers. He is waiting for them to choose Him.

There is incredible power in choosing to submit to the Holy Spirit for truth in the pursuit of freedom from darkness. When persons who have lived much of their lives in confusion realize that Jesus will honor their personal choices, the road to healing becomes much smoother. There are, of course, many times when an abuse survivor will not choose to submit to the Holy Spirit. This can be quite frustrating for prayer ministers, but it is a fact of ministry that cannot be underestimated. The transformation of an abuse survivor cannot be hurried. We must operate within the parameters established by the person's choices. We must be sensitive to the process.

You Can Help—with the Right Tools

I have written this book to help those who want to bring the healing mercy of Jesus into the despairing and confusing world of the traumatized. Even though it is difficult to help someone recover from the wounds of abuse, we can do so with confidence because it is the heart of our heavenly Father to set the captives free. I believe that He desires to heal survivors so they can feel His love for them and know His direction for their lives. It is the job of prayer ministers, then, to lead the captives into His presence. We can help these hurting ones know the truth about our Father, and discover their destiny in His Kingdom.

This is my passion: to minister to those scarred by abuse, to help those cowering in the darkness of confusion and pain come out into the light of God's love. I want people to see that whatever kingdom they focus on is the kingdom that has the most power in their minds. If an abuse survivor focuses on Satan and the lies believed during times of trauma, then the bondage and darkness continue. If, however, a survivor learns to focus on the freedom that our Father offers, freedom is available. *Any hurting individual who chooses to submit to ministry and who trusts the person who is gifted in this kind of healing can be set free.*

Romans 12:2 says that we are transformed by the renewing of our minds. This should be the goal of inner healing ministry to abuse survivors: to help them change the way they think so that they can know the truth about our heavenly Father. This will be the basis of our study.

Abuse survivors often feel stuck in their spiritual journeys. Those praying for them often feel frustrated by what appear to be unnecessary stops on the road to healing. Waiting on a person to choose to submit to inner healing—whether it involves repentance, forgiveness, renouncing a vow or judgment, or listening to the Holy Spirit—is a ministry challenge. It is usually a slow process, but persistence will pay off in the end. We must be patient and let a person's pain do its work. More often than not, by the time individuals come for inner healing ministry, their pain will cause them to submit to Jesus for healing. We can be patient in our part of the process because we know that our heavenly Father is faithful to release healing and freedom to all who choose to come to Him.

Although I focus on abuse survivors, the information here can help you minister to anyone who desires to receive freedom and move forward in his or her spiritual journey. I believe that if we are equipped to minister to the extreme dynamics of abuse, we can minister successfully to those suffering from other abuses.

I want to give you hope that real healing does happen, and it happens frequently. I also want to tell you to be realistic about the difficulty you may encounter as you pray for someone to find—and stay on—the road to healing. These individuals have lived in a war zone for most of their lives. Hope and patience will keep you in peace as you lead them into the light of God's truth.

2

A Simple Approach

The most challenging thing I have ever done is work with people who have been so traumatized that they have been left with multiple personalities. Today this condition, once known as *multiple personality disorder*, is referred to as *dissociative identity disorder*. One of the most helpful explanations of how this happens to a person is offered by Dan Allender, author of *The Wounded Heart: Hope for Adult Victims of Childhood Sexual Abuse* (Navpress, 1990).

> Dissociation begins when reality is too distasteful or traumatic for us to bear, we disconnect from what is present and flee to an illusory world of our own creation. The power of dissociation is that it involves both flight and imagination. Flight involves a refusal to trust that, within an awful moment or event, God or good is to be found. Then it involves the powerful experience of making a new world that is to our liking and control.

If you pray with hurting people, it will not be long before you pray with someone who has been traumatized by abuse. Many, many people in our world are hurting. They may have suffered because of abusive parents or caregivers. They may have endured neglect or loss. They may have, like Bob, been the subject of ritualized terror and formed personalities to handle the pain. In each case, whenever a person has suffered trauma and believed lies of the enemy, he or she needs help connecting with the Father for cleansing prayer and to learn God's truth. In this chapter we will begin to look at the basic structure of ministry to help accomplish this.

As I mentioned in the last chapter, prayer ministers should not be making any clinical determinations, including regarding multiple identities. If you find that this seems to be a likely diagnosis of a person you are praying with, I encourage you to place your trust in the Father to guide you as you pray. You might explain that trauma causes small children to separate from pain, and that process often results in different personalities or parts. It is important to let the person know that you are not making a diagnosis, and that if she wants a professional diagnosis she should seek the assistance of a Christian psychotherapist or psychiatrist.

I do encourage you, however, to assure the person that you can continue to pray for him and allow the Holy Spirit to heal and bring wholeness to his soul.

The people I have ministered to with this disorder feel shamed when they realize that they have multiple personalities. They are also threatened by the diagnosis of dissociative identity disorder. This is usually because they are misinformed about the meaning of *dissociation*. When they think of DID or multiple personalities, they think of hopeless crazy people locked away for life in insane asylums. We have all seen movies like *One Flew Over the Cuckoo's Nest* or *Sybil*.

At the very outset I try to remove the shame and fear of this diagnosis. I speak directly to their fear of being labeled and tell them they are not crazy or broken beyond repair. Anyone who endured childhood abuse has some defense system in place.

People are much more comfortable when we use the term *fractured* or *fragmented mind* to describe what they are experiencing. This is a term that can be related to a broken or divided heart. They tell me that when I explain things in benign terms that apply to everyone who experiences trauma, they are comforted. It encourages them to move forward in prayer. People with fragmented minds are actually using very creative defenses: It takes an imaginative mind to form these helpful personalities, as well as to keep the fragments from uniting or letting themselves be exposed.

Working with people who experienced trauma, in any degree or form, demands a great deal of patient kindness on the part of the person praying for them. Let me begin, therefore, by reminding you that nothing is impossible for God. Nothing is too complex for Him. I have seen Him set many people with fractured souls free.

Understanding the Effects of Abuse

When trauma begins in infancy, people are robbed of the ability to process pain. They cannot interpret what happened to them correctly. Young children misinterpret violent abuse by personalizing it. They usually conclude that it must be their fault. The enemy then can take advantage of lies that children believe about themselves and intensify their pain.

Abused children are also left with an incomplete capacity to distinguish danger from safety. This creates a blurred sense of safety that often leads to further abuse. Abused children can be manipulated easily because the scars of abuse have distorted their sense of self.

When children are weak and vulnerable and unable to understand why bad things happen to them, they default to disconnecting from reality. In some cases, children create a fantasy life where everything is good and nice. Because violent abuse is overwhelming, those who endure it often deny that it ever happened by hiding it in their minds. This is dissociation, and it is a natural response to childhood abuse. Survivors who resorted to dissociation often try to convince me that they were violated only once, and that they were old enough to remember all of the details. This usually is not true. A fragmented mind is usually the result of years of trauma.

I keep my explanation simple enough for a child to understand, and explain that there are degrees of dissociation. Everyone who has ever been caught daydreaming during a boring lecture has experienced dissociation. It is common for dissociation to be more extreme when abuse begins in early childhood and continues for years. I relate the term *extreme* to the number of fragmented personalities within a person's mind, the functions of the personalities and the person's awareness of their internal personalities.

There is a wide range in the number of personalities a traumatized person might have. Some have a few main personalities, and others tell me they have hundreds. The personalities can have various jobs. Some, for instance, protect the painful memories that contain the details of abuse. Others have specific jobs that help the person function in daily life. Some people tell me that they have a religious personality who goes to church, reads the Bible and can talk about Jesus. They believe that they need a religious personality to present a normal Christian life because they were ritualized in mock Christian settings and have great internal fear about God, Jesus and the Holy Spirit.

Those considered to be extremely fragmented have personalities that perform jobs they are not aware of. One man told me that he has college transcripts that verify high performance in subject areas that he does not know anything about. One woman told me that friends saw her at a restaurant and enjoyed chatting with her, but she does not remember going to the restaurant, how she got there or how she got home. When personalities function independently of the person's awareness, the professional classification is *amnesia*.

In prayer ministry, both a simple internal defense system and an elaborate internal defense system can be resolved by the healing power of the Holy Spirit. This is a comforting truth for fragmented people, who become anxious when they realize they have multiple personalities. It releases hope when I tell people that I have seen many extremely fractured minds made whole by inviting the Holy Spirit to tell them God's truth about what happened to them and the lies that they believed.

Because a fragmented mind distorts one's true identity, it is understandable that these individuals are confused about who they are. And when people are confused about who they are, they forget many things about themselves. They forget what makes them happy. They forget what they like. They forget about their talents. When a fragmented person forgets who he is, he tends to describe his sense of identity in different ways. He might say that he feels like many different people at the same time, or he might say that he does not feel like a person at all.

This leads to another coping mechanism. Because survivors do not feel "real," they compensate by presenting to the world a false self in order to be accepted or to be able to function with all of the unresolved pain inside. This *false persona* is generally created from a composite of fragmented personalities, is patterned after someone that the person likes, or is an expression of behaviors that the person perceives to be acceptable. More on the false persona in a moment.

When a person's mind believes lies about abuse, the lies become the lens for interpreting life. The lies lay the foundation for every belief; the beliefs develop systems; the systems construct a mindset. Renewing the mind is the solution for a traumatized person.

Helping trauma survivors discover who they are is a crucial part of their healing. In fact, until a person's identity is established with truth and not lies, his mind will remain fragmented and he will continue to live life from a false self. Dissociation—a fragmented mind—is resolved by truth. Survivors can be assured that when God tells them the truth about their abuse, it will make sense and they will no longer feel the inner need to hide it.

Retraumatizing the Hurting

Trauma survivors frequently begin our ministry sessions with feelings of hopelessness. The battle in their minds has been going on so long and is so intense, and the abuse that caused it was so severe, that it seems too good to be true that something as simple as prayer could bring peace. This hopelessness is often connected to past experiences of reaching out for help and being retraumatized by those in positions of authority.

Survivors of spiritual or sexual abuse were usually violated by those in positions of spiritual authority over them. Fathers, mothers, older siblings, even pastors have abused children entrusted to their care. In occult abuse the abusers pretend to be pastors, priests or representations of our heavenly Father or, as we see in Bob's case, Jesus Himself. They frequently wear costumes during times of abuse while speaking lies about our Father, Jesus and the Holy Spirit, knowing that they are creating personalities in the victim's mind. This staging can be simple or elaborated in great detail. But the result is the same: The victims of this kind of abuse fear God and His representatives.

This leads to a very important principle of helping the abused: Be exceptionally careful not to retraumatize the individual. Believe it or not, those in positions of spiritual authority often speak words to abuse survivors that are harsh and judgmental. Many spiritual leaders are ignorant of the damage this kind of abuse can do to the human personality. Even a well-meaning pastor or spiritual director who does not understand the dynamics of trauma, and particularly of a fractured soul, can cause additional harm.

I prayed with a young woman who was the victim of extreme occult abuse inflicted on her as a child by adult authorities. Joyce, now grown, was aware of her internal personalities and the specific behavior of many of them—some of whom became angry around authority figures. She cried as she told me that several pastors whom she contacted for help disbelieved her story and attributed her dysfunctional behavior to sin in her life. Unwittingly these pastors were reinforcing the points that her abusers made during the abuse: God is mad at you because you are a bad person. They thought that she was a willing participant in a satanic sexual ritual, and finally concluded that she was a witch. Unfortunately this is not an uncommon response by pastors when they hear a story of this kind of abuse.

When these statements provoked the anger of a child-personality within Joyce, the pastors assumed this behavior was demonic and began to pray deliverance prayers. Those who are unaware of the results of long-term mental, sexual, physical, spiritual and occult abuse often treat internal personalities as demonic spirits. Joyce felt hopeless as they tried to cast demons out of her.

It was not that she had no demons; she did. I have never met a person who experienced satanic ritual abuse who did not have demons. But the angry little girl speaking from within Joyce was not a demon; it was a fragment of her personality. It did not need to be cast out, but to be integrated back into her personality; the demons would be dealt with separately. Sometimes the demons are cast out after the integration, sometimes before. It all depends on the person and the leading of the Holy Spirit. The pastors, not understanding any of this, were actually bruising an already brutalized young woman. Jesus was careful and gentle with the bruised (see Isaiah 42:3).

Joyce came to me for ministry, but since I was in a position of spiritual authority, she did not trust me. We met together several times before trust was established and she was willing to listen to what I had to say. I spent time building a relationship with her by allowing her to voice her fears and frustrations. I talked to the personalities, telling them that Jesus understands when children are angry about being tricked and abused. She later told me that she appreciated my allowing her time to feel safe before we began prayer ministry. Abuse survivors often use the term *safe* to refer to people, relationships or environments that they believe will not lead to abuse.

I want to be real when I tell you about ministering to abuse survivors. It is not always as successful as it was with Joyce. Several years ago another young woman came to me for prayer ministry. She had also been abused in an occult environment, and she had the same resistance to those in authority. She did not trust anyone. I understood her struggle and began the process of building a safe relationship.

This woman decided that she wanted to relocate to the town where I live to take advantage of intensive ministry time. She attended the church I attend, and engaged in the home group my husband and I lead. We occasionally went to social events together. My daughters embraced her and shared their lives with her. We spent many hours in ministry and additional time processing her healing journey. This continued for three years.

During this time period there was always tension: She believed that I was going to deceive her at any moment.

She never fully trusted me. She could never provide me with a reason why she did not trust me, but she did not. A three-year, intense inner healing journey ended when she decided that I was just like the people who had abused her, and she left town. Her hopelessness and fear were stronger than her willingness to trust me.

Hopelessness is the logical result of being labeled or diagnosed with something that a person believes cannot be healed. I tell abuse survivors that it is important not to agree with any diagnosis that our heavenly Father does not agree with. I ask permission to lead them in a prayer to break the agreement with any label that is in conflict with how our Father views their situations. Most people agree with this prayer. I explain that words have the power to curse or bless (see James 3:10), and that I want to pray words that bless. I then pray blessings over the person's mind and body. When a person feels blessed, she feels hope.

Jesus' Uncomplicated Approach

It is encouraging to remember how Jesus heals. In response to a withered hand, Jesus says, "Stretch out your hand!" (Matthew 12:13), and the man is restored. In response to a woman's twelve-year hemorrhage, diagnosed by numerous physicians (she probably had many diagnoses spoken over her), Jesus proclaims her healing (see Matthew 9:20–22). In response to a demonized man, Jesus says to an unclean spirit, "Come out," and the man is in his right mind (Luke 4:33–35). In response to a troubled heart or confused thoughts, Jesus says, "Believe in Me" (John 14:1). It is often just this simple: Come to Jesus and be healed.

I tell abuse survivors who have dissociation that all of the personalities within their minds can simply come to Jesus. I encourage the personalities to choose Jesus, for Jesus is the only one who can heal them. He is the only one who can give them life, forgive their sins, and heal their hearts and minds. I remind survivors that Jesus knows the specifics of their abuse and that they do not need to remember the details before they come to Him. Many personalities feel trapped because they believe they do not have options. It releases hope when they realize that they can make this choice.

Let's return to Bob's ministry time. Through this encounter you can see that our goal at this point is to get the person and the personalities within the person simply to come to Jesus.

Showing Bob the Truth

Bob had spent years denying the internal personalities, voices, confusion and gender struggles. I explained to Bob that when the mind does not embrace what actually happened, then that particular fact, that particular truth is being denied. Denial is always connected to functioning without truth. (I will discuss denial more fully in the next two chapters.) I encouraged Bob to believe that the path to freedom is truth and reality. Denial and truth cannot reside in the same place.

Jesus' answer to a fragmented mind begins by replacing denial with reality. He replaces lies with truth. These two Kingdom principles are essential tools in healing the scars of abuse.

Bob finally admitted that he had lived in denial for many years. He now understood that with the love of Jesus he could embrace the fragmented parts of himself in a way that would dissolve fragmentation and lead to wholeness. He learned that receiving truth about abuse resolves mental confusion and leads to peace. His mind was becoming whole.

This did not happen in one ministry session, of course. Here is an overview of four points that helped this broken part of him come to Jesus.

Tell the Personality about Jesus' Love

Bob told me he had decided that if he were a little girl perhaps Jesus could still love him. Then, choking back tears, he said, "But He doesn't love the little girl. She is dirty, too."

I talk and pray with whatever personality the person presents. There is always a reason why a specific personality manifests at an exact time. I simply ask that personality why she decided to talk to me. When I asked the little girl this, her childish voice came from under the blanket: "I don't think there is any way that Jesus could love me."

I told her that I cared about what she had to say, and that Jesus would tell her the truth about whether or not He loved her. I almost always say something like this to encourage the person and to explain that Jesus can help, if the personality wants His help. I have found that whenever the personalities speak to me, it is because they want help. This is an encouraging step because it means the bond of trust has begun to form.

I tell the child personalities that Jesus loves little children and wants them to know the truth about what happened to them. Jesus does not like it when bad people hurt little children and lie to them while they are hurting them. I connect this with what the person shares with me about how he or she was hurt. When I asked the little girl why she was bad, she told me how the men had raped her and told her it was her fault. They told her that this does not happen to good little children. Bob was so young when this happened, the little girl personality believed what the men told her.

I began to tell the little girl how Jesus told His apostles to bring all the little children to Him (see Luke 18:15–17). Child personalities like to hear Bible stories, even if they feel that they are too dirty for the story to apply to them.

I told her that Jesus wants little children to tell Him about what is making them sad. Child personalities usually argue that they cannot talk to Jesus because they are dirty. This always refers to sexual abuse and the shame that makes them feel forever disqualified.

The story had hit home, however. The little girl wanted to talk to Jesus and told Bob so. But she also said that she feared Jesus would not talk to such a bad, dirty girl as she. I suggested that we ask Jesus the truth about that statement. Bob, who was speaking now, agreed to this but was very afraid of what Jesus might say. He wanted to stay under the blanket. I assured him that he could hear Jesus under the blanket.

Ask Jesus to Speak to the Personality

I prayed and asked Jesus to speak to the little girl, and then I waited. Slowly the blanket came down. Bob had a look of astonishment on his face. More tears flowed as he reported the little girl's words. She told him that Jesus said the man who hurt her had lied to her. The little girl said that Jesus did not think she was bad or dirty, and He was sad that she was hurt. She said that the bad man played a trick on her, and Jesus does not like tricks; He always tells people the truth.

I suggested that we ask Jesus the truth about being a little girl.

Ask the Holy Spirit to Speak Truth to the Person

I prayed for the Holy Spirit to tell this personality the truth about her gender. We sat in silence for two or three minutes. Then Bob said, "The girl knows she is a boy and that pretending to be a girl did not keep her safe because she was hurt many times after that."

The little girl no longer spoke. Before me now, in Bob's body, was a little boy. I asked the little boy if he could see Jesus inside. He could. I encouraged him to see if he felt safe enough to stay close to Jesus. He said that it felt safe, and he thought it was a good idea.

Invite the Personality to Connect with Jesus

Bob was once again present and communicating with me. He was encouraged because he now had hope that the conflict over his gender could be resolved. It was also the first time he felt safe with Jesus and knew that Jesus really loved him. I explained to him that regardless of the number of personalities, the degree of mental, physical, sexual, spiritual or occult abuse, the answer is the same: Invite the personalities to connect with our heavenly Father, Jesus and the Holy Spirit to receive truth about the abuse.

Bob agreed but was worried that he did not know the right kind of questions to ask Jesus concerning the abuse. This is common among abuse survivors. I said that it was not important how the questions were asked because Jesus knows everything that happened to him. He knows about the tricks, the details, the lies and the scars from the abuse. The important thing is to trust Jesus to speak to him.

I explained to Bob that he had access to every part of his mind, and that he had the ability to communicate with every part of himself. Within fragmentation, each one of the personalities keeps the memory of the abuse it experienced secret from the other personalities and the adult. I use simple language to describe the need for the adult conscious person to know what happened to the personalities inside.

I told Bob that as soon as he was willing to embrace the truth that every fragmented personality was part of him, wholeness could begin. There is a tendency for the adult or core part of the abused person to reject fragmented personalities that know painful things about abuse. They often want to deny fragmented parts that are angry, curse, or hate God and other people. As soon as the survivor is able to embrace every fragmented personality in his mind as a true part of himself, the healing process will accelerate. This is easier to say than to do. The separate personalities came into being through an attempt to escape pain. Welcoming them back means admitting the reality of the abuse and acknowledging the shame that always comes with it.

Bob believed that I was being honest with him and chose to accept the fragmented parts of himself. He invited the personalities, their pain and their stories to become part of himself again. He said that he needed a few moments to talk to the various personalities. He closed his eyes as if he were praying, and told me that the personalities understood the process of going to Jesus for truth.

Bob then "felt" various personalities gathering together within him, almost like a family reunion. Several of the voices became one voice. For the first time he could remember, he felt peace.

Dealing with Internal Groups of Personalities

Once the principle of coming to Jesus is realized by the wounded person, it is tempting to think that ministry to other fragmented parts will be quick and easy. This is not necessarily the case, and it can be discouraging to prayer ministers and survivors alike who witness an initial breakthrough. The principles are consistently effective, but the actual application of the principles can be slow. Within a fractured mind there are often groups of personalities. We deal with the personality or personalities that manifest.

Although Bob reported a new level of understanding, he now realized that he had groups of childlike personalities within him. He initially thought he had only a few personalities. Even though he knew these things, Bob became discouraged about the number of personalities that surfaced. I reminded him that Jesus would set all of them free just as He had set the little girl free, and he was comforted by that thought.

Bob learned that different personalities represented specific times of trauma. He told me that many of the personalities loved and trusted Jesus. Yet, even though some of them loved Jesus, they were in denial about what had really happened. Some of them did not acknowledge that they were abused. Some of them thought the abuse was their fault. Some of them thought that they were bad and deserved the abuse.

We dealt individually with each personality that manifested and the lies that personality believed. We ended the day with many personalities receiving truth and freedom. This created a group of personalities that trusted Jesus. Since all the fragmented parts inside can hear what is going on, I encouraged anyone else who wanted help to go to Jesus also. I always tell the personalities that are still hidden that nothing they have survived, seen or done disqualifies them from going to Jesus.

I also prayed and asked the Father to shine His light into any place or on any hidden personality in order to show the path that leads to Him. Many people tell me afterward that when I pray that prayer many of the hidden personalities actually see how to get to Jesus.

The child parts that are with Jesus can be very helpful in ministry. Looking at Bob, I suggested that the personalities now trusting Jesus tell the others about Him and encourage the others to listen to Him. I suggested that the ones that felt compassion for the unhealed personalities go and comfort them. This is a valuable tool for ministering to numerous personalities at the same time. Groups of personalities can hear that the Kingdom of God belongs to them, and that the bad things that happened to them do not disqualify them.

I continued to minister to Bob until he felt whole and no longer confused. We weaned our ministry sessions from every other week to once a month. Presently we get together once or twice a year for prayer. He knows the truth about his occult abuse and openly shares his story about how Jesus healed him from the scars of abuse. He no longer struggles with gender confusion. He is in a more intimate place with Jesus than he has ever known.

Bob encourages other survivors that Jesus is the answer to their pain. He has a powerful testimony.

True Identity and the Heart's Desires

I have never met a traumatized person who was confident in his identity. Because layers of fear generally mask the abuse survivor's true identity, it becomes normal to create a false self—a *false persona*—that serves the purpose of acceptable presentation. In other words, survivors try to look and act like nice, normal people in order to avoid further rejection. Their abuse left them with extraordinary rejection—rejection by their abusers, rejection by other people who did not understand their pain, and even rejection of themselves. Survivors believe lies that tell them it is unsafe to expose any aspect of who they truly are.

This is an important aspect to explain in the beginning hours of ministry sessions. Survivors need to know up front that we realize we are interacting with an artificial presentation of who they are. I usually explain that our true identity is based on who God says we are. Psalm 139:14 is an excellent assurance: "I will give thanks to You, [Lord], for I am fearfully and wonderfully made; wonderful are Your works, and my soul knows it very well." God designed them uniquely. When they realize who they are and feel good about who they are, they will be positioned to live confidently in their true identity.

I also explain that true identity is connected with the desires of their hearts. Healing will not change someone's personality; it will, however, remove lies and defensive behaviors, allowing his or her authentic personality to be released. In order to help survivors understand the importance of their identity as Christian believers, I suggest that they read Neil Anderson's material on identity in Christ. This helps them gain a true frame of reference for who the Father says they are.

Sometimes I tell survivors that I understand the abuse left them feeling insignificant, but that God says they are significant (see 1 Corinthians 3:9; 4:1–2). I tell them that the Father created them to do great things. It is best to keep this simple: If they do not know who they are or what they can do, they cannot do it. When they know who they are and what their gifts are, however, they can implement them because the truth activates what abuse hides.

Abuse dismantles a person's ability to dream. Brokenhearted people are disconnected from all that they long for. I believe that desires cannot be separated from true identity. It is a major goal in the inner healing process to help the traumatized remember the desires of their hearts.

I usually ask people very early in their healing journeys to list things that they like—both what excites them and what breaks their hearts. I have them rewrite the list again after several months of ministry. It has been my experience that the things listed that excite people are connected to their gifts and talents, and the things that break their hearts are related to their destinies.

Perpetrators lie to the abused about their abilities; prayer ministers have the opportunity to speak truth. Abusers speak death to those under their control; prayer ministers have the power to speak words of life. Proverbs 18:21 says, "Death and life are in the power of the tongue, and those who love it will eat its fruit." Our words have the power to nurture the brokenhearted and give life to them as we lead them to Jesus.

A few years ago I had a dream that I now understand reflects my own heart's desire to pray for abuse survivors. I was on a ladder in a deep, dark hole. The bottom of the hole was crowded with people whom I was reaching for. The ladder below me was barely visible due to the darkness. If I looked down into the hole, I could not see anything, but if I looked upward, I could see light. The light was coming from Jesus. He was lying on the ground extending His illuminated hand into the hole for me to grab. If I looked away from Jesus, I did not have enough light to help anyone climb up the ladder.

This dream reminded me that we are not very successful in leading survivors out of bondage on our own. We must keep our eyes focused on Jesus and allow Him to direct the ministry. Jesus will direct us as the Father is directing Him (see John 5:19). When we are tuned in to the voice of God and are friends with Jesus, the words that we speak to others represent Him. The Father knows the true identity of every person who is hidden under scars of abuse. He loves to grant the desires of their hearts and release them into their destinies (see Psalm 37:4).

Stay in Tune with Jesus

Prayer ministers who are in the position of spiritual authority need to be personally committed to inner healing and transformation. My husband and I are committed to inner healing. It is a regular part of our lives. We pray with each other when we encounter anything in our lives that begins to rob us of our peace in Jesus. Every three months we have a healing weekend with our dearest friends who share the same commitment to transformation. We spend three days in our home where we share meals with each other, discuss what the Father is doing in our lives and pray with each other. We fit in a few walks and an occasional movie, but our agenda is inner healing. We have an established routine. In the afternoon, the women pray together and give Jesus permission to resolve the issues that are hindering our lives. After our evening meal, all of us spend time in conversation with the goal of inviting the Holy Spirit to search our hearts for anything that He wants to tell us the truth about.

I honestly could not suggest inner healing to others if I were not committed to it in my own life. An emotionally healthy prayer minister, who delights in his or her life with Jesus, is in a position to encourage hopeless people to choose the hard work required for the process of inner healing.

Abuse survivors who have lost touch with reality and want to die need a healthy prayer minister. Prayer ministers need to be happy people who love life. When I meet a counselor who is depressed and lacks passion for life, I doubt his effectiveness in helping others find joy. It reminds me of a marriage counselor who has been divorced several times trying to instruct others on how to stay married. We need to be equipped to give survivors the courage to choose life. Prayer ministers must be in tune with Jesus and walk in the joy of the Lord. We are in a ministry position to encourage others to choose life, not death; we need to be people who enjoy life. Many abuse survivors have a refined ability to discern when an authority figure is being dishonest. I am not saying that prayer ministers cannot have a traumatic past. I am saying that they need to be healed and healthy and confident in the Father to lead the brokenhearted successfully. It is a wonderful picture of healing, deliverance and transformation when a person who is healed from the scars of abuse in turn leads others to be restored.

Jesus said that in the world we would have trouble, but in Him we would find peace (see John 16:33). Working with the wounded does not have to be complicated. If we stay close to Jesus and follow His example of caring for the brokenhearted and downcast, we will see Him work a miracle of peace in their lives.

3

Looking at Fear and Denial

Many people who come for prayer ministry often do not know why they need help. They sense that something is wrong because they feel stuck in their ability to live healthy lives. Some might say simply that they cannot make good decisions or think clearly. Others might talk about bizarre behaviors that they cannot explain or control. The behaviors include addictions that they hate, waking up in strange places and not knowing how they got there, having several different handwriting styles in their daily journal entries, being paralyzed with fear in response to normal smells or sounds, and cutting themselves with knives or other sharp objects when they feel anxious or experience a change in schedule. They want help—in many cases they trust God for the help—but they are frightened because they have such "weird" or dangerous behaviors.

Jesus says that a divided kingdom or house cannot stand (see Matthew 12:25). Since the Kingdom of God is within the human heart and mind, a divided mind can be compared to a divided house. When confused individuals come to me for ministry but are unaware of the source of their odd thoughts or behaviors, I talk to them about the possibility that memories might be hidden in their minds. I explain that things are hidden away because they are painful—and they will stay hidden until we are able to process them with truth. I try to help these individuals understand that there is an explanation for their strange behaviors.

Beginning to Look at Denial

It is common for a dissociated person to have unusual reactions to certain stimuli and not remember the trauma behind these behaviors. They are using a strong defense mechanism called denial. Denial begins when some truth is too painful to accept. It is an efficient method of hiding in the mind the painful, unresolved things that one cannot make sense of. It allows the truth of what happened to the person to remain lost.

Survivors need help in order to stop denying the things that are hidden away. In fact, if they try to figure it out on their own, their protective and defensive thoughts will interfere. They need help to see that the Holy Spirit is the only one capable of showing them what they are denying, when they began denying it and the reason they are denying it. As they submit to the Holy Spirit, He will search out whatever is important for them to know and open to remembrance places that were once forbidden.

Whenever someone is confused or fearful about irrational behavior, I suggest that we begin by asking God about its source. People who are in denial often forget that our Father knows all of their secrets. Psalm 26:2 is a helpful passage to read in this instance: "Examine me, O LORD, and try me; test my mind and my heart." David further asked God to expose any anxious thoughts in his mind. Psalm 139:23 says, "Search me, O God, and know my heart; try me and know my anxious thoughts."

I suggest the person pray and ask God to search her mind for anything that is being denied or hidden. As I pray for her to see her trauma, she begins to remember hidden things. This is her first step toward understanding the selective amnesia of dissociation.

It often occurs that once a person is aware that there are hidden or dissociated things in her mind, another wave of anxiety arises because she does not know what else may be hiding in the recesses. Once again I encourage her to seek God for the answer. I continue this pattern until she is no longer afraid.

The Common Scar of Survival

Within the divided house of a survivor's mind, walls of defense are common. Again, it is helpful to use the term *fragmented* or *fractured* rather than *dissociated*. When I am explaining fragmentation I usually relate it to trauma experienced in childhood. A little child's brain is not mature enough to process abuse; therefore, the child must separate himself from the pain. This is the beginning of an abused child's method of surviving. I let survivors know that there are often times when the pain is hidden so well that they have completely forgotten about it. This ability to stow memories away is referred to as *compartmentalizing*, and the contents of the compartments are different for each individual.

People are creative in their ability to hide pain within their minds. They might create rooms, boxes, maps, systems or detailed structures in order to separate from what happened to them. I usually encourage them to tell me what they know about their hidden pain. I do this to see if they have completely buried their abuse history. Some people experience emotional pain but are disconnected from the memories attached to it. Some people remember what happened to them, but they have no feelings about the trauma. They have numbed the pain. The dynamics of denial in a fragmented mind vary from individual to individual.

People often want to deal with the walls of defense—to open the rooms, boxes or compartments within their minds—but they are unable to do so. As we begin to pray and ask God to help them remember what they need to remember, they encounter resistance. This resistance is related to fear.

All walls have fears attached to them; it is common to be anxious about remembering things that have been hidden for many years. The fears cannot be disregarded. The person needs to know the truth from God in order to break through.

Exposing Fear

Prayer ministers must be patient with a person's unwillingness to take down the protective walls. We must operate within the parameters of the person's will. We never direct the person to answer in the way that we feel she should answer or suggest what we think God might be telling her. Here are three steps that have proven helpful in dealing with a wall of defense:

First, I ask the person if she wants to take down the wall. If she says yes, I ask if I can pray for her. I then ask God to tell her the truth about the wall. If the person says no, she does not want to take down the wall, I ask what it would mean to her if the wall were removed. This question usually exposes the person's fear. If the person you are praying with is not ready to look at any walls of defense, then remember throughout this process that we are always directing the person to our Father for truth.

Second, once the person tells me that God has encouraged her through prayer that it is safe to let go of the wall, I ask what she wants to do. Hearing the truth from God does not always mean that she will choose to do what He says. Often the person's fear is greater than her trust in God. God will not violate her personal choice; neither should we.

Third, when the person realizes that she has a fragmented mind, the next step is helping her understand the importance of working toward wholeness. She must realize that there is hard work ahead to break down walls of defense. It is helpful to assure the traumatized that when their minds are made whole through truth, the scars of abuse will be healed. They will no longer feel the need to hide things.

Hard work is an inescapable part of the inner healing process. Trauma alters a person's view of reality. It often weakens her desire to work hard. For victims of abuse, *normal* means "survival." Their wills have been so crushed by their abusers that they usually are not willing to do the hard work of processing trauma memories and breaking through the denial. Honestly, I must tell you that this has been a major battle with every abuse survivor I have ever known. Their abusers have been successful in making them think and feel like helpless victims. It is not unusual for them to drop out of the healing process and claim that they can become whole on their own.

When I see survivors pulling away from the hard work of breaking down walls of defense, I challenge this deception by asking them if what they are doing is working. It amazes me that they frequently answer yes. The usual response to this distorted view of reality is to point out the bizarre behaviors that they are struggling with. I might ask why, for instance, they are still cutting themselves, if their time alone with God is healing their scars of abuse.

Freedom from the bondages of abuse requires help. If they could have gotten free by themselves, they would have been free a long time ago. They need help to overcome the fear of facing what was done to them. They need help to feel the love of God. They need help to do the hard work of healing the past wounds. They need help to see the lies that they have believed for years. I have never seen or heard of anyone at this stage in his journey getting healed from severe abuse on his own.

The healing process is painful for these individuals, and will probably be the hardest work they have ever done. Making this clear to them is simply being kind and truthful. Many spiritual authority figures mislead the traumatized about what it takes to heal the scars of abuse. All anyone has to do, they say, is believe in the resurrection. This lie causes additional pain to those who love God and have spent hours in heartfelt prayer, and yet are still trapped. Prayer ministers should offer spiritual solutions that help people process their pain without inflicting on them a sense of failure. Our goal is to help the traumatized create new realities based on truth.

Even when a person is ready for the hard work it takes to find freedom, the process of becoming whole can feel overwhelming. People often cry and tell me that they feel hopeless. This is a natural response for those who live in despair: Anyone who has sought help for years and not gotten it is likely to be depressed. In my years of working with people who have multiple personalities, I can remember only four people who were not on antidepressants.

In their search for healing, survivors often put their hope in a type of therapy or a particular therapist, but when hope is based on a human being, disappointment is inevitable. Only when our hope is rooted in our heavenly Father can we have assurance of a good future.

Correctly Placed Hope: In the Father

The greater the denial, the stronger the walls of defense, the more divided the house, then the greater chance that those seeking help have not experienced freedom. When the walls of defense are strong, when a person has sought help for years and has not been set free, depression leads many survivors to retreat from healing. I define *depression* as "the loss of hope." When people are consumed by the painful side effects of abuse, they lose hope. They disconnect from good things. They have no vision for the future. They are stuck in a place that makes them want to die.

The depression that cripples them is, in my opinion, spiritual in nature. This means that the answer to hopelessness and depression is also often spiritual in nature. Our job is to lead them to the presence of the Father where they can feel loved.

I received a phone call for help recently from a person trapped in the evils of drug use. I began by asking if I could pray for her, but as I began to intercede she hung up on me. We repeated this cycle a couple of times until, finally, she told me that there was no reason for her to live. She had lost any vision of a positive future. She was hopeless. I made arrangements for her to be admitted into a short-term rehab facility because she did not want spiritual help. She did not know that God is our only hope.

If those seeking our help do not believe that there is an answer to their pain, we cannot help them. God is the only one who will not disappoint us. Romans 8:28 tells us that hope is the confidence that our ultimate future will be good because God's plans and purposes for us are always good. It is at the heart of inner healing to encourage people to choose to trust the Father and place their hope in Him in order to end their battles with depression.

Listen to how David survived years in the wilderness, being chased by a king who was insane with jealousy and determined to kill him:

> To you, O Lord, I lift up my soul; in you I trust, O my God. Do not let me be put to shame, nor let my enemies triumph over me. No one whose hope is in you will ever be put to shame, but they will be put to shame who are treacherous

without excuse. Show me your ways, O LORD, teach me your paths; guide me in your truth and teach me, for you are God my Savior, and my hope is in you all day long.

Psalm 25:1–5, NIV

No matter how bad things got, David and the other psalmists never stopped believing in the goodness of God. One of the great confessions of the goodness of God is found in Psalm 119:68: "You are good, and what you do is good; teach me your decrees" (NIV).

Ministry—One "Slice" at a Time

I believe that our Father has a specific desire every time we meet with people for prayer. He knows the big picture concerning their redemption, yet He is sensitive to where they are in their journeys and what defensive walls are blocking their progress at that particular moment. We need to be sensitive as well. We can pray with confidence that God will heal whatever they are willing to yield to Him.

Jesus said that He is the bread of life (see John 6:35). I often use this Scripture in my prayers before a ministry session. Because Jesus is the bread of life, I ask the Father to give me bread for the person I am preparing to pray for. When we pray in this way, we are asking our Father to give us the aspect of Jesus that the person needs. We trust Him with the details of the ministry session.

Even though it is typical for people to say in their first ministry sessions that they want to receive everything Jesus has for them—right now!—survivors generally feel as though they do not have the energy to deal with years of hidden trauma. Wounded individuals, even though they want to move along quickly, can feel overwhelmed during ministry times.

Most people do not eat an entire loaf of bread at one time. We understand how much food is needed per meal and how often we should eat. This is the time to slow things down and consider only that "slice" of bread that they can digest. Generally this means to process one memory at a time. This should initially be a memory that the person suggests and is comfortable sharing.

Transformation is a process. Tina's story is a good example of the benefit of slowing things down.

Tina's Story

Tina's husband contacted me shortly after she was released from a psychiatric hospital. She had been depressed and was cutting herself. Tina was hurting herself in an attempt to stop her internal pain. She could not figure out why she was falling apart. Her husband told me that her latest episode had scared them both. Tina had disappeared for an entire night. She had awakened in a nearby park the next morning and did not know how she had gotten there. Fear had led her to me.

Tina was very intelligent. She was beginning to put a few pieces of her puzzled life together through her personal research. She looked at me intently and said, "I think I have multiple personalities; I just don't know why." She continued to tell me that she did not have time for years of therapy because she had a family to take care of. She said she felt overwhelmed at the thought of processing years of trauma, even though she was not aware of any trauma.

Tina understood that multiple personalities are a result of long-term abuse. She also wanted me to know that she thought she had some personalities that were doing things she was not aware of. She looked like a librarian as she peered over the top of her eyeglasses and said, "That means that I have some degree of amnesia. That is what it means if I have personalities that do things that I don't remember."

I shared my thoughts with Tina about slowing things down and processing one memory at a time. I suggested that she choose what she was comfortable talking about.

Since she was still upset about the unknown details of awakening in the park, she wanted to process that event. Then she looked at me and said harshly, "And don't tell me what *you* think Jesus should be saying to me about this!"

I responded with a surprised, "Excuse me?"

She explained in curt tones that her last prayer minister had mixed the ministry of the Holy Spirit with New Age guided-imagery practices. She stopped going to that counselor when she recognized that the process was being diluted by her counselor's interference.

Tina was correct in her understanding of the principles of inner healing. I assured her that I follow the leading of the Holy Spirit, that in our prayer times together, the Holy Spirit would tell her the truth about the lies in her mind. I agreed with her assessment of inner healing ministry, and restated that the ministry of the Holy Spirit is pure only if prayer ministers do not speak for God or guide what the person should be remembering. Prayer ministers must be committed to staying out of the way and allowing the Spirit of truth to do the leading.

Tina was satisfied with this, and requested that I pray for her by asking the Father the truth about how she got to the park. I sat there thinking to myself that she might have amnesic fragmented personalities, but her faith in God was strong. Tina interrupted my thoughts to say that she did not care what she had forgotten; she believed that Jesus would tell her the truth and heal her mind. She said that she loved Jesus and knew that He is the only answer for her freedom.

The Lord Searches the Heart

As I prayed for Tina, the Holy Spirit confirmed to her that she had personalities who were doing things independently of her awareness. Tina began to understand that amnesia allowed a fragmented part of her to go to the park. At that point, Tina remembered receiving a phone call, and a man asking to talk to a little girl part of Tina named Paige. It was Paige who agreed to meet the man in the park. Tina remembered the man's voice: He was one of the men who had molested her.

The Holy Spirit searched Tina's heart and enabled her to remember the beginning of her traumatic life. Her abuse began at birth and continued for many years. Tina was asking for the truth about that one aspect of her life—how she arrived at the park—and the Father was revealing the truth.

As she processed the memory, more information came to light. The phone had rung three times and stopped.

This happened a second time a few moments later. Those series of rings reminded Paige that she was the one who was supposed to answer the phone. As I continued to pray for Tina, asking the Holy Spirit to reveal the truth to her about her going to the park, she told me that she understood how the part of her named Paige agreed to go to the park and meet this man. Tina remembered he had threatened her if she did not do whatever he said whenever he called. Tina remembered being sexually abused several times by the man who whispered in her ear that he would kill her family if she did not obey him when he called her. The fragmented part of Tina named Paige agreed to keep the family safe and obey the bad man.

Tina was glad that she chose to slow things down and focus only on her major concern the first time we prayed. The few years we spent together processing her traumatic history confirmed my initial thought about her faith in God. She made courageous choices in most of our ministry sessions and displayed consistent trust in the Father.

Tina's choice to receive the Father's truth during her inner healing journey led her to wholeness. The amnesia within her mind was healed, and the fragmented parts within her mind were united. At that stage, she developed the ability to process—on her own with Jesus—any latent memories that surfaced.

Even though survivors need help breaking through denial and fear, they can, as they move into wholeness, develop the ability to process memories independently. This is actually an important goal in leading them to freedom. It takes time, but everyone has the potential to get to the place where this is possible. This is significant because these individuals need to develop a life with Jesus outside of their relationship with their prayer ministers and counselors. Those we pray with need to become dependent on Jesus, not us.

Tina finally understood that the Father is good. She told me that she always believed that He was good, but now she had personal healing experience to match her belief about Him.

We talk on a regular basis. She tells me that her intimacy with God continues to grow. She is enjoying her healing and shares her story with others. In addition, she is refining her communication skills and no longer suffers from debilitating introspection. She is able to adapt to changes that come into her life. She tells me that she is experiencing joy.

These are all signs that I use to define wholeness, freedom from fear and denial. Wholeness comes with the understanding that calling on the name of our heavenly Father heals the scars of trauma. This is what the Scripture says:

"I love You, O LORD, my strength." The LORD is my rock and my fortress and my deliverer, My God, my rock, in whom I take refuge; my shield and the horn of my salvation, my stronghold. I call upon the LORD, who is worthy to be praised, and I am saved from my enemies.

Psalm 18:1–3

Working within One's Level of Ability

As we pray for the wounded to turn to the Father, we must remain alert to the parameters in which He would have us minister. Even though, as prayer ministers, we are in the "business" of offering hope, it is very important that we operate only within our scope of experience and ability. I am not trained, for instance, in the area of drug and alcohol addiction; thus, I never agree to minister inner healing with those who are trapped in substance abuse. I tell them that I will be glad to offer ministry to them after they complete a drug or alcohol rehab program.

Let me use substance abuse as an example of knowing when to make a referral to another individual or agency that specializes in areas of help that we cannot offer.

It is fair to say that people with substance addictions believe many lies. It is also appropriate to assume that they need inner healing to expose the root of their addictions. I feel confident in saying that most substance abuse is the person's attempt to numb pain that is trapped in his heart. The effects of drugs and alcohol, however, interfere with the person's ability to be honest about what he is feeling, thinking and doing.

Early in my ministry, before I made the inner resolution not to pray with someone who is an active substance abuser, I prayed with a man who was an alcoholic.

Ralph was not a survivor of ritual abuse, physical abuse or any form of sexual abuse. His life, however, was a wreck. The first time I met Ralph he looked as though he had not eaten or slept in months. The dark circles surrounding his eyes, coupled with the frown on his face and his extremely thin body, told me that he was carrying great pain. He told me that he was not able to hold a steady job. He said that he was a Christian and that he loved Jesus, but that he felt as though Jesus was far away. He had not attended church or interacted with healthy people in years because he did not want to be around anyone who was happy.

I asked Ralph how I could help him. He said he had heard that I prayed for people and helped them with pain.

Ralph told me that he had been an alcoholic for many years and that it had destroyed his life. I asked him when he began drinking and if he could remember what was going on in his life at that time. He skirted the issue by telling me that he had been drinking for so long and so much that could not remember anything. I asked him what he felt when he was not drunk. He told me that the shame that he felt was so intense that he had to drink.

Ralph stated emphatically that he had not had a drink for one year. He told me that he had entered a rehab program two times in the past, but he quit when it was time to talk about the shame that he felt.

I told Ralph that I believed that the Holy Spirit would help him understand his addiction as well as the reason he felt so much shame. Ralph was open to prayer, and the Holy Spirit brought to his mind the tragic car accident many years before that had killed his wife and children. I prayed and asked the Holy Spirit to help Ralph understand why he felt shame when he remembered the accident. I would have expected Ralph to feel grief about such a painful situation, but shame seemed out of place in the story. Ralph began to cry and would not look at me. I asked him if there was anything that he wanted me to know. He continued to cry and look downward. We met for prayer several times before Ralph told me the rest of the story.

I remember the day that Ralph came into the prayer room at church, began to cry and told me that he was driving the car when the accident occurred that killed his family.

Through my own tears I asked Ralph if I could pray and ask Jesus to talk to him about the accident.

Jesus told Ralph that it was not his fault. Jesus told him that it truly was an accident, and that He wanted Ralph to stop blaming himself. Ralph seemed transformed, with a smile on his face as he told me that he had a strong sense that his family was with Jesus. He told me that he saw a picture in his mind of his family in a peaceful place with Jesus. I asked Ralph if he was ready to forgive himself and stop trying to punish himself. He agreed.

I thought this would lead Ralph to regain control of his life. I thought he would begin sleeping, eating and talking to people. I felt confident that he would never return to drinking. I was wrong.

Ralph continued to come for prayer ministry and finally confessed that he had never stopped drinking—and that he was still drinking. Aside from my frustration that he had lied to me, I was confused. I knew that Jesus had spoken healing words of truth to Ralph, but he was still drinking. I prayed and asked the Father to tell Ralph why he was still getting drunk. The answer was not one that Ralph wanted to hear. The Father made it clear to Ralph that he needed to enter rehab and that he needed to complete the program. I suggested that Ralph allow my intern and me to drive him to a local rehab facility and that he make a commitment to me that he would complete the program. Ralph agreed.

Ralph completed the program. He realized that the chemical dependency in his physical body had to be addressed in order for his mind to have the capacity to receive the truth that Jesus spoke to him. Ralph is doing great.

Every Sunday he approaches me in church with a big smile and tells me about all of the good things that are going on in his life, including a return to work.

We both learned that his healing journey out of fear and pain would have been much easier if he had dealt with his alcoholism first. This taught me the importance of prayer ministry boundaries, working on the level of one's ability and experience, and the wisdom of working with other professional resources.

Beauty for Ashes

Isaiah 61 shows us a great picture of redemption. It is a picture of a healing cycle that can be used to encourage people who need a vision for a future that is free from fear and denial.

People who have difficult pasts often believe that they can never contribute to the Kingdom of God. Isaiah tells us differently. The brokenhearted can be set free, restored and positioned to receive good things from our Father, which they can then share with others in need: "The LORD has anointed me to bring good news to the afflicted; He has sent me to bind up the brokenhearted, to proclaim liberty to captives and freedom to prisoners" (verse 1).

When people realize that the abuse they endured was so severe that it shattered their minds, they tell me that hearing a Scripture about the Father healing their wounds is comforting. Ritual abuse leaves a person feeling trapped in darkness because the abuse occurred in a very evil environment. When I read this Scripture, it is common for people to tell me that they feel like a prisoner because they feel alone. They appreciate that this Scripture says specifically that God wants to proclaim liberty to the captives and freedom to prisoners. They receive the blessing of the Father setting captives free.

People receiving ministry always seem to enjoy it when I tell them that our Father likes to exchange good things for bad things.

> And the day of vengeance of our God; to comfort all who mourn, to grant those who mourn in Zion, giving them a garland instead of ashes, the oil of gladness instead of mourning, the mantle of praise instead of a spirit of fainting. So they will be called oaks of righteousness, the planting of the LORD, that He may be glorified.
>
> Isaiah 61:2–3

It is exciting to know that God desires to exchange beauty for ashes and joy for sadness, as these are things that most people desire. But survivors often have no grid for understanding the goodness of the Father. This wonderful idea of exchange actually creates tension for those who do not understand that good things can be theirs.

It helps, when this tension arises, to encourage survivors to identify what they would like to exchange. A good way to do this is to give examples of negative emotions that are commonly connected to abuse memories. Simply remind them of the emotions that they have asked God to heal. They are very familiar with painful feelings such as sadness, despair, depression and hopelessness. Survivors smile when I tell them that God wants to exchange these negative emotions connected to pain and bondage with the opposite positive emotions associated with healing and freedom.

Part of the reason they struggle with these things, of course, is that abused people often hold the heavenly Father responsible for their abuse or for not rescuing them. They begin their healing journey with a false view of the Father, Jesus and the Holy Spirit. Helping survivors overcome lies about God is a major part of the inner healing process. It is important that we teach those we pray with about the goodness of God and His desire to rebuild all that was destroyed by the evils of abuse.

Survivors tell me that Isaiah 61 encourages them. They like the fact that this Scripture says that God wants to do more than heal them; He wants to bless them and transform them beyond recognition to those around them. He wants them to experience a joyful life:

> Then they will rebuild the ancient ruins, they will raise up the former devastations; and they will repair the ruined cities, the desolations of many generations. Strangers will stand and pasture your flocks, and foreigners will be your farmers and your vinedressers. But you will be called priests of the LORD; you will be spoken of as ministers of our God. You will eat the wealth of nations, and in their riches you will boast. Instead of your shame you will have a double portion, and instead of humiliation they will shout for joy over their portion. Therefore they will possess a double portion in their land. Everlasting joy will be theirs.
>
> Isaiah 61:4–7

I witnessed this transformation in Rita. Rita moved to my hometown to receive inner healing ministry. As a child, Rita had been sold to several different families over the years for the purpose of sexual abuse. Rita was scarred by sexual, physical, spiritual and ritual abuse. Rita was repulsive to those around her. She had a bad attitude about everything. She was angry. She was rude. She was demanding. She played the victim card daily. She had no understanding of interacting with others in an appropriate manner. She did not have a grid for joy.

I read Isaiah 61 to Rita shortly after we started prayer ministry. She said bluntly, "Well, that sounds good, but I don't believe it." She informed me that a sex object is never viewed as righteous. Rita had many fragmented child personalities who believed they were valuable only for sex.

Rita manifested a rude, seductive, tough-girl attitude, but I quickly learned that it was masking her shame. I asked Rita if she wanted to know what God thought about her. I assured her that He already knew everything about her abuse. Rita proceeded to put on another layer of bright red lipstick and answered angrily, "I already know what He thinks of me. He thinks I'm dirty. He thinks I'm bad. He doesn't like bad girls."

It took several weeks before Rita agreed to allow me to pray for her and ask God to tell her the truth about herself. We spent many weeks after that praying and listening to the Father's truth. Rita's attitude began to soften a little. She acted a little less seductive. She began to dress a little more modestly. She was less angry. Rita gradually acknowledged that God cared about her, and she came to believe that He cared about justice. Glimpses of joy began to replace Rita's harsh attitude. She told me that she was beginning to believe Isaiah 61.

Rita moved out of the area before her healing was complete. I no longer have contact with her, but I am thankful that she experienced the heavenly Father's desire to break down the dividing walls of fear and denial that kept her from knowing Him.

Survivors of abuse often feel separated from the Father. They are devastated by the evil that has robbed them of so much of their childhoods. Walls of fear and denial keep them in darkness and bondage. But when they learn that our heavenly Father desires to break down those walls of defense and heal the scars of their abuse, they understand that redemption can truly be theirs.

4

Houses with Many Rooms

It is common for people who have fractured souls to describe their internal structures like a house with many rooms. Different personalities occupy specific rooms. Donna is a case in point.

Donna's Locked Rooms

Donna sat serenely on the couch in front of me, looking as if she had stepped out of a fashion magazine. She had elegant posture; her folded hands and her crossed ankles reminded me of a beauty pageant contestant. Her hair, nails and makeup were flawless. Her tasteful clothing reflected a female who was very focused on appearance. She spoke with confidence as she told me of her academic accomplishments and her successful life.

Then, in the middle of her attempt to convince me of her many abilities, she began, with an abrupt change in demeanor and voice tone, to contradict everything she had just said.

Donna's body language became masculine as she parted her legs, leaned forward and rested her elbows on her knees. She frowned as she looked at me and spoke in a harsh, deep tone. She said her name was Faith, and she proceeded to tell me that Donna was a liar because her life was a mess. Although Faith was a fragmented part of Donna, she was not in agreement with Donna's perspective on life.

Faith told me emphatically the "truth" about what was going on inside of Donna's mind. She explained that many girls lived in the big house with numerous rooms. The rooms were arranged according to the stories of the girls who lived in them. Faith wanted me to understand that the word *stories* referred to the way each girl was abused. Faith said that Donna knew about only a few of the girls and a few of the rooms.

Donna shared a room with other glamour girls. Faith rolled her eyes as she repeated the term *glamour girls* because she had her own negative opinion of them. Faith said Donna and her friends fixed themselves up and acted confident in order to seduce men. Faith told me that Donna referred to herself as glamorous, but she knew Donna to be a whore. She was glad that their rooms were not close together and that they did not communicate with each other because she was nothing like her host.

I met many different girls who were fragmented parts of Donna and who wanted to tell me their stories. I learned that the rooms with the most painful memories had the strongest locks on the doors. The most shameful rooms had girls assigned to stand guard, keep silent and make sure the door remained closed. The intricate structure within Donna's mind contained many personalities unique to their trauma. As Faith began to trust me she introduced me to many other residents inside. As trust was established, some of the girls felt safe enough to open their doors.

Donna's abuse took place in an occult environment, so many of her rooms represented lies about Jesus. Before Donna and the girls trusted me, she refused to allow Jesus to enter the house. She said no when I asked if I could pray for her, because she was convinced that Jesus took part in her abuse. She told me that many times when the evil people were violating her they would laugh and say that Jesus could save her if He wanted to. She had many rooms that were off-limits to Jesus. My experience with Donna was the first time I learned that abused people sometimes create an internal fantasy that appears as a house.

Building a Desirable House

Scripture also uses the analogy of building a house, but in this instance, of course, it describes the goal of a godly and fruitful life. The foundation for this house is Jesus Christ Himself. First Corinthians 3:10 tells us that this desirable house is built on solid ground and constructed of quality materials: "According to the grace of God which was given to me, like a wise master builder I laid a foundation, and another is building on it. But each man must be careful how he builds on it."

Abusers weaken a person's mind, causing, as with Donna, internal construction to hide fear and shame. A strong mind, however, builds with true beliefs. When a person does not understand how God strengthens the mind, I turn to Proverbs and compare strengthening the mind to establishing a house. Establishing a house follows the construction and includes things that make a house a permanent home. Proverbs 24:3–4 says, "By wisdom a house is built, and by understanding it is established; and by knowledge the rooms are filled with all precious and pleasant riches."

As I have noted, survivors view transformation as a quick spiritual act. They ask me frequently if I know anyone who has a spiritual anointing to pray for fragmented minds. I believe that our heavenly Father is quite capable of integrating a fragmented mind supernaturally and instantly, but that does not lessen the importance of being honest with people at the beginning of their healing journeys and not promising a time frame. As we have seen, transformation, like good construction, takes time. Developing a strong, healthy mind entails commitment.

People who seek help want to build strong minds. They submit to ministry because they are tired of living with fearful thoughts. Their internal structures, built to escape the pain of reality, take a lot of time and energy to maintain. The quality of life for these individuals has been diluted by confusion. As prayer ministers, we should lead the brokenhearted to the Spirit of wisdom where they can learn to establish their minds in the ways of the Father.

Prayer ministry should stress the importance of learning to process life with God's truth. A divided mind is not established in truth. We should help survivors cultivate a sound mind that is under God's influence. "For God has not given us a spirit of timidity, but of power and love and discipline" (2 Timothy 1:7). Truth strengthens a weak mind.

It might sound too simple, but people tell me that comparing the construction of a house to the ongoing work of healing their minds helps them. Most people agree that the construction of a house is a process and that the process is sequential—from laying the foundation to incorporating the finishing touches that make a house a home. This allows us to talk about the stages of healing a history of abuse, and the fact that replacing lies with truth is the foundation for reconstructing a godly mindset.

And it does not stop there. We can assure those in need that the heavenly Father will not only direct their "construction," but will continue to guide their steps, leading them into the work that is best for them. As prayer ministers, we help survivors develop confidence that God will direct their paths for all of their lives: "Trust in the LORD with all your heart and do not lean on your own understanding. In all your ways acknowledge Him, and He will make your paths straight" (Proverbs 3:5–6).

The Goal: Building Relationship

As I look out my upstairs window, I have a direct view of the house that my son-in-law is constructing. Before he and my daughter began the foundation for their house, they held a time of prayer on their land and asked God to bless it. They prayed that the house would be a place where the Father would dwell, a place where others could experience His presence and receive healing and deliverance. This reflects my son-in-law and daughter's desire that their physical house become an established home.

Although my daughter and her family are anxious to dwell in their new home, the steps of construction must be sequential. Building a house is a process. Inner healing is a process. It is important for people to approach inner healing with the goal of strengthening their spiritual lives with God. Many pursue healing solely for the purpose of relieving their emotional pain. While we must be sensitive to a person trapped in pain, I suggest that our goal be focused on knowing God. Our greatest purpose is leading the brokenhearted to a place where they can realize the ways of the Father. Remember these words from Psalm 139:23: "Search me, O God, and know my heart; try me and know my anxious thoughts; and see if there be any hurtful way in me, and lead me in the everlasting way."

It amazes me how many times people are surprised when I discuss the connection between inner healing and a close relationship with the Father. Individuals who are struggling with the dynamics of a fractured soul are commonly confused about God's will for their lives. They often confine God's will to a very narrow, religious path. Most tell me that they are supposed to be a missionary, preacher or prayer minister. Many people act surprised when I suggest that after they are healed they might have a different perspective about their life with God. Sarah did.

A New Perspective on Life

The first time Sarah walked into my office I thought she must be an artist; at least she looked like my image of an artist. After listening to her tell me about her life's story, I was convinced she was an artist. She told me about her childhood abuse and her adult struggles in an extremely poetic manner. Then she handed me a book of poetry that she had published and requested that I read a few pages. I honored her request and read several pages. I was amazed at Sarah's ability with words. She was a gifted poet. Then she tossed a CD over to me that had a beautiful picture of her on the front playing a guitar, and she suggested that I listen to it during our lunch break. It also was amazing. My initial view of Sarah was correct. Sarah was a multitalented artist.

I proceeded to affirm Sarah's artistic giftedness and wondered aloud if God would be leading her to pursue a career in the arts. She shook her head and insisted that when she was healed she knew God wanted her to be a prayer minister. At that point, I kept my thoughts about her artistry to myself, but the image of this wonderfully expressive person choosing a career that largely involved listening and silent prayer made me smile.

I did ask Sarah, though, if I could give her my general opinion on the matter of ministry. She agreed. I told her that whatever career she chose, inner healing releases people to establish their lives with God. Trauma sometimes leads people to over-spiritualize the Father's will. This is because the scars of abuse often distort a person's identity and ability to connect with God in a real and intimate manner. I suggested to Sarah that she might have a different perspective on many things after she received inner healing ministry. She shook her head. She was sure that God would heal her in order for her to enter full-time ministry.

Sarah and I spent several months together in prayer and inner healing ministry. Her healing was obvious. She became relaxed. She started talking about Jesus with a new language. She described her relationship with Him as a friend, someone she trusted. She began telling me that she knew God loved her. She even told me she knew that He was responsible for her gifts and talents.

Most mornings Sarah would walk into my office and hand me a new poem or song that she had composed the night before. Her giftedness was increasing. Periodically I asked Sarah if she thought God would approve of her pursuing a career as an artist. Sarah would respond with a smile and say, "Perhaps."

Sarah decided that she was in a peaceful place and chose to stop prayer ministry with me. Her scars were being healed and she was slowly becoming happy. I prayed for Sarah and blessed her future. Among other things I prayed that she would know God's will for her life.

Sarah did not keep in contact with me, but a few years ago I saw a new book of poetry that she had published. I also learned that she had released a new CD and was traveling and singing. Sarah's inner healing allowed her to develop a friendship with Jesus and released her to build her house on that sure foundation.

The Strongest House

As prayer ministers, our goal is to help desperate people build a relationship with God. The Bible tells us that the purpose of renewing the mind is to position us to know God's will: "Do not be conformed to this world, but be transformed by the renewing of your mind, so that you may prove what the will of God is, that which is good and acceptable and perfect" (Romans 12:2).

Ultimately, our role as prayer ministers is to represent Jesus. In order to tell others effectively about an intimate relationship with the Father, we must speak from personal experience. The more connected we are with the presence of God, the greater the love we will have for those who need our help.

In order to lead traumatized people to develop an established spiritual life, our view of transformation must reach beyond integrating a fragmented mind, relieving trapped emotional pain and resolving the consequences of abuse memories. It must be focused on pursuing God. Then we can pray with confidence in our heavenly Father's ability to help them build strong houses and heal the scars of their abuse.

5

What Do You Want Jesus to Do for You?

Jesus asked two blind men who were calling out for mercy what they wanted. Their condition was obvious, yet Jesus asked them to state it (see Matthew 20:30–32). It is always good practice to follow Jesus' example, so I often ask people what they want Jesus to do for them. A person's answer reveals his willingness to process abuse memories. It helps the prayer minister understand who is serious about letting God break down the walls of defense and who is not.

Lorrie knew about her sexual abuse long before we were introduced. She sat on my worn floral couch and told me calmly that she had been in therapy for years. She had processed many painful memories of her sexual abuse—hard work that was helping her understand how her mind responded to her childhood trauma. She realized that she had buried the painful memories deep inside and forgotten about them for many years until she decided to pursue therapy.

Lorrie was talking so fast, chattering on so nervously, that I was unable to ask her Jesus' question, or any other for that matter. She finally stopped for a breath, and I started with the basics, asking her why she had come to see me. She told me that she could not figure out why some sounds were still triggering certain actions and feelings within her.

Lorrie then explained further. When she heard drumbeats in songs, for instance, she experienced some of the same feelings she had felt during her times of abuse. Lorrie was confused by this because she believed that she had been healed of her trauma during her previous therapy sessions.

Lorrie attended a church that played contemporary worship music. Many of the worship team members were men. Lorrie told me that she felt guilty about it, but that when this music was playing she could not engage in worship without experiencing inappropriate emotions. Lorrie said that all through the worship time either she was crippled by fear or she struggled with shame because every song made her feel sexually aroused.

I asked, "Lorrie, are you willing to process some additional memories?" She responded positively but said that she was a bit nervous. I assured her that it was very normal to be nervous.

I then asked Lorrie the important question: "Lorrie, what do you want Jesus to do for you today?"

She got a puzzled look on her face and said that I had asked her an unusual question. I could tell by the serious tone in her voice that she was thinking about how she wanted to answer.

Lorrie perked up, smiled and said, "That is a great question." She began her answer by explaining to me that her previous therapy, which was traditional cognitive therapy for her sexual recovery, provided her with insightful coping skills, but her pain was still trapped inside.

She paused, and then stated that she wanted Jesus to do two things. "Well, I want to know why I feel weird when I hear music, and I want to know why I am afraid of men." She elaborated by telling me that as a little girl she could never understand why she had "weird" feelings when she was around men. As early as preschool, Lorrie remembered feeling afraid when men were close to her. She told me that she also felt as though she was supposed to take off her clothes when she was with men or she would get into trouble. She continued in an uncertain tone. "I don't understand this," she said, "but I think the music issue and my fear of men are connected."

Lorrie wanted Jesus to heal her so she could enjoy an entire church service. She wanted Jesus to restore her ability to engage in worship. Lorrie chose to trust the healing process and submit to the work of the Holy Spirit. She asked me if she could have a blanket with which to cover her head before I prayed for her.

I began by praying and asking Jesus to answer the desires of Lorrie's heart. I felt compassion as I saw Lorrie try to escape from her shame under the blanket, and I thought how sad I would be if I could not listen to the worship music that I loved.

I kept my prayers simple and waited patiently for Lorrie's response. It was very quiet in my office for a long time. As I sat in silence I was reminded about connecting with the Father when we are still. I opened my Bible and let my eyes fall on the words of Psalm 46:10, "Be still, and know that I am God; I will be exalted among the nations, I will be exalted in the earth" (NIV).

Lorrie slowly lowered the blanket until I could see that she was crying. She just sat there staring at me and crying. Finally Lorrie stated, "I get it. It all makes sense now. I know why I am afraid of men. I know why I feel sexually stimulated when I hear music. I know why I have always felt that I was going to be punished if I didn't take my clothes off."

I asked Lorrie if she wanted to talk about it. She said that she would like to take a lunch break. I was not sure she would return.

Lorrie did come back after lunch, and she was ready to discuss her revelation. Lorrie told me that she remembered being sexually violated numerous times by men who were playing worship music. As each man took his turn violating her, he would threaten to kill her if she did not agree to take off her clothes and not resist him when she heard the music. Lorrie looked at me through teary eyes and said that she did not understand why anyone would be so cruel to a little girl. She said that Jesus told her that it was not her fault, and that she had no reason to feel shameful. She told me that she had a sense that Jesus put a white fluffy dress on her that made her feel clean.

I prayed for Lorrie and asked Jesus to restore everything that was stolen through her years of abuse. I specifically asked Jesus to help Lorrie experience His peace when she is around men and prayed for her to enjoy worship music. I have not seen Lorrie for several years, but I smile whenever

I hear about her leading worship at her church or at a conference. Asking someone what she wants Jesus to do for her reveals her willingness to explore the very depths of her bondage or find a few answers that will calm her pain. Not everyone who comes for ministry is serious about being healed. We must acknowledge that transformation is unique to each person. Some pursue healing with great intensity; others need to be gently encouraged to move forward. Others resist any movement toward healing. Let's look at examples of breaking down the walls of resistance to Jesus.

"Yes, but..."

Frequently people will say that they cannot remember their abuse, even though their stories contain clear evidence of what happened to them. Many times as I listen to their stories, I think that what they need is obvious. Sometimes people really do not connect the dots; they really do not consciously remember. Sometimes, though, they are consciously choosing not to look at the situation that brought them in for prayer ministry.

I can recall at least ten women who have sat in my office and shared their "obvious" stories with me. Every story contained red flags that indicated sexual abuse. They told me details about their inability to have sexual relationships with their husbands. Most of them felt shameful and dirty. Some of the stories even included flashbacks of someone holding them down while they were crying out for help.

The women all admitted that something was wrong with them. They acknowledged that they should be able to enjoy sexual intimacy with their husbands. When they read a routine question on my intake form about child-hood trauma, however, the women had the same dramatic response. "I am not going there. I know what that means." Each woman had a "yes, but" response to getting help. It does not make sense to me, but women often tell me that they would rather live with their internal, trapped pain than be labeled a sexual abuse survivor. They tell me that keeping their internal screams silent has become normal. Their preconceived view of ministry for sexual abuse prohibits them from receiving healing.

I asked each woman the same question: "What do you want Jesus to do for you today?" Their answers indicated their unwillingness to surrender to the Father and trust that He would tell them the truth. Most of them said, "I want the nightmares to stop, *but*" or "I want to be able to enjoy my husband sexually, *but*" or "I want to be happy, *but*." Each woman wanted help, but each woman was afraid to remember any abuse. Each woman initially said yes to inner healing, and then attached a restriction. "Yes, but" blocked the path to healing.

I define a "yes, but" as anything a person is unwilling to release. I became aware of this response when I kept hearing people say that they wanted healing for an issue, then contradict themselves with a fearful thought about acknowledging the reality of what they were asking for.

"Yes, but" can be an insightful tool. Whatever a person is not willing to let go of is always attached to fear. Fear is always attached to lies. I respond to "yes, but" by asking the question, "What are you afraid of?" I sometimes rephrase the question and ask them what it would mean to them if their "yes, but" were true. This question often reveals the person's fear or lie about their resistance. A person's list of "yes, but" items can be lengthy, but none can be overlooked.

Dorothy was a fifty-year-old professor. She was an intelligent Christian believer who professed to trust God. She had a husband, adult children and grandchildren. Dorothy appeared to have a successful career and a healthy family unit.

Dorothy began her story by telling me that she needed help. She said that she did not want to live with the torment that she was experiencing. Dorothy would become fearful whenever her husband touched her in any way. At first I thought she meant that her husband was abusive. She clarified that he was a very gentle and kind man. She was afraid of his hugging her, holding her hand or sitting close to her. I asked Dorothy to continue to describe what was tormenting her.

Dorothy became very anxious as she started to tell me about her sexual life with her husband. She dropped to the floor and curled up in a fetal position as she continued to tell me about her pain. Dorothy said that she would begin to shake when she saw her husband without clothes; she would become tense and unresponsive during sex; she would cry hysterically after sex; and she would have violent nightmares after every sexual act with her husband. Dorothy said that she also frequently saw demonic spirits in her house that would paralyze her with fear.

I asked Dorothy if she was aware of any abuse in her background, and her demeanor changed quickly. She got up off of the floor, wiped her tears and said that my question was totally out of line. She then stomped out of my office.

Dorothy is a good "yes, but" example. She wanted her pain and torment to stop, but not if it meant anything that she did not want it to mean.

This is very frustrating to me. I want to be honest with you about how discouraging it is to see someone in so much pain who is not willing to surrender to Jesus for healing. To watch fear control a person's life is heartbreaking. We need to encourage people to have surrendered hearts. We need to encourage people who are controlled by fear to ask Jesus to help them.

Understanding Separation from God

Survivors' defenses ("yes, buts") often block their desire for close fellowship with the Father. It is common for abuse survivors to tell me that they feel disconnected from God. They read the Word, they listen to worship music, they attend church, they pray, but there is still a wall. Survivors often believe that God speaks to people. They believe that He speaks words of truth and life to people's minds (see Matthew 4:4; John 6:63), but they cannot hear Him.

There are many reasons why abuse survivors who want to experience the Father's presence feel separated from Him. Demonic spirits, unforgiveness, sin, hatred and curses are a few common explanations for their feeling disconnected from God. As we have noted, their walls are frequently built of fear. They are afraid of what the Father will want them to remember. They are afraid that the Father will want them to remember something that they want to deny. This can be frustrating for the prayer minister. The individuals say one thing but do another. They are sad because they cannot build a relationship with God, yet they are unwilling to open up to Him.

When a person sitting in front of you says that she wants to experience the presence of the Father, she means it; the fragments of her personality, however, do *not* want to experience the presence of God. A fragmented part of the person is generally responsible for this kind of block. A specific personality is resisting God and defending a lie.

Many prayer ministers respond to this situation with words and behaviors that tell the abused person they do not believe her. This, of course, is not helpful.

It is being loving when we can help an abuse survivor understand how her defenses are keeping the truth out. Survivors are often surprised when I tell them that I believe they want to connect with the Father and develop an intimate relationship with Him. I affirm that there is a reason for their resistance. I ask them if they are willing to allow me to talk to them about what some of those reasons might be.

Inner healing is a two-way process. Our Father is the one who heals; for our part we must choose to receive from Him. We need to make sure that survivors understand they have a part to play in their healing journeys. When a person sitting in my office is hesitant to allow me to pray for her, I might suggest we break for coffee or lunch and spend some time just talking. No one likes to be alone when feeling stuck. Healing has many facets; many people appreciate simply the chance to talk.

Remember, though, that we cannot move beyond the person's choice. If she does not give me permission to deal with the wall, we are at an impasse. I get frustrated when a person chooses to leave with the same wall that she came in with, but I have to give her the right to choose.

Many people ask me what I do when a person ultimately says no. When that happens, I tell the individual that we cannot proceed until he is willing to open up. I let him know that I am not giving up on him, but that I must operate within the confines of his personal choice. Jesus will not violate his choice; therefore, I will not violate his choice. A person's healing journey is based on his decision to submit to the transforming work of the Holy Spirit.

A Core Violation vs. the Details

Let me mention here that while some survivors do not want Jesus to reveal any details of their abuse, others tend to seek His revelation on these particulars to the point of obsession.

The core violation must be uncovered and confessed, but it is not necessary to ferret out all the details, the incidental parts of the abuse. By core violation I mean the key element of the experience. If a person was abused, for instance, he needs to embrace it. If he was abused by a family member, that is an important detail that the person must own, or he will continue to identify falsely the one who abused him. That kind of falsehood negates the complete truth and, therefore, freedom. If a person was abused by a stranger, for instance, but she hates her father and accuses him of the abuse, this is not truth and cannot lead her to freedom. These are examples of important details. An unimportant detail might be the color of the room where the abuse took place.

Trying to recover every single detail of the abuse can complicate the inner healing process. Where the abuse took place, how often, how many people were in the room—all of these are natural questions for a survivor to ask, but trying to answer them can be a distraction from healing rather than an aid. I have found that the Holy Spirit will bring to light the necessary details. I often have to remind survivors that truth is the answer to their healing and health, not remembering every aspect of what happened.

Some things that were done to some of these people when they were children were so horrifically evil that they feel no one would even speak to them if they knew their awful secrets. In these cases, it is necessary for the abused ones to tell another human being what they experienced in order to receive healing (see James 5:16). They need to tell their secrets to a loving person and feel the compassion of God come through that person to them. When a survivor tells the worst secret of her life and sees love in the face of the person listening to her instead of revulsion, it is usually the beginning of her healing. She is then able to bring her heartfelt prayer to Jesus.

Ellie: It Comes Down to Choice

"What do you want Jesus to do for you today?"

Along with providing insight into people's willingness to move forward in ministry, as well as revealing any fear that is keeping them in bondage, this question also helps survivors make plans. Asking those with whom you pray what they want, and writing it down for them, gives them a record of their progress. It is encouraging to survivors, who feel as though their healing journeys will never end, to be able to look at their notes and see that the Father is healing what they asked Him to heal.

Ellie was a recovering alcoholic and drug addict. She said that the drugs and alcohol had made the pictures go away for a while, but now the flashbacks were getting more and more detailed. She wanted me to help her make them go away when she was not under the influence.

She had begun to recognize the men in the flashbacks who were taking turns raping a little girl. She recognized her priest. She recognized her uncle. She recognized her dad. She could not see the little girl's face, though—and she made it clear that she did not *want* to see the little girl's face.

Ellie began to twist the pillow she was holding, and her face deepened in shades of red that seemed to match her increasing anger. "I just want them to stop!" she shouted. "I don't know why I need to know about someone being raped!" She told me that she wanted me to help her get rid of the demons that were responsible for the pictures in her mind.

I asked, "Do you want to know the truth about the pictures in your mind? Do you believe that Jesus will tell you the truth? Are you willing to take responsibility for whatever the Father says you need to take responsibility for?"

She answered yes to all of my questions. I explained to Ellie that there was a reason why she was seeing the flashbacks. I wanted her to understand that there was a connection between them and her life. She was an intelligent person and understood everything I said to her. She assured me that the connection made sense to her, but she did not know how or why.

I then asked, "Ellie, what do you want Jesus to do for you today?"

Her answered surprised me. She said that she wanted to know who the little girl was.

I said, "Do you realize that you are making a choice to allow our heavenly Father to tell you the identity of the little girl in your mind?"

She answered, "Yes. I have to know." I prayed and asked God to tell her the identity of the little girl. We sat in silence for a few minutes. Then Ellie said that she did not hear anything from God. I ask her to close her eyes and tell me if she saw anything.

She told me that she saw the same picture that she had been calling a flashback, but this time it was not going away. The picture remained in her mind. She said it was the same one that she had been trying to get away from by getting drunk. She still saw her priest, uncle and father in the picture sexually violating the little girl. "I still can't see the little girl's face," she said.

I repeated my question, "Do you want to see her face?"

"Yes," she said.

I prayed in agreement with Ellie's choice, and asked God to tell her the truth about the little girl. Ellie began to gag. She dropped her head and began to heave in the trash can at the end of my couch. When she could speak, she attempted to tell me what her body was experiencing as she looked at the picture frozen in her mind: "I can feel my body being sexually stimulated."

Ellie must have thought that I did not understand her because her voice grew louder. "I mean my body is feeling that now, while I am in this room!" Ellie was yelling now.

I told her that there was a reason why her body was feeling what her mind was seeing. I encouraged her to ask the Father what was happening in her body.

I prayed for her, but before I could ask her anything she screamed, "I am feeling what the little girl is feeling. *The little girl is me!* I recognize my dress that is on the floor. It was my favorite dress." I told her that God had answered her prayer because He loved her and wanted to heal her. She did not hear me, either because she was crying and screaming, or because she was blocking out what I said.

When Ellie calmed down I asked her if I could pray for her again. I prayed a simple prayer and asked Jesus if there was anything else He wanted her to know. Ellie broke the silence with her crying. I asked her if she was crying because she was happy or sad. She did not answer me. She kept her eyes closed and kept saying, "That is so sweet, thank You, Jesus."

In a few moments she looked up and told me that Jesus came into the picture in her mind and picked up the little girl. He wrapped her in a soft blanket as He held her and told her that He loved her.

Ellie looked at me and asked what had just happened. I explained to her that the flashback was a memory that had surfaced. What she had experienced physically is called a *body memory*. Pain and trauma can be trapped in the physical body as well as hidden in the mind. We will talk more about healing of the physical body in chapter 9.

Ellie was thankful to know the truth about the flashbacks that were wrecking her life. We spent the next few years processing the trauma that was locked in her mind and her body.

My ministry to Ellie was determined by what she was willing to ask Jesus to help her deal with. The time we spent together in prayer was based on her personal choice. Ellie's initial intention was to receive ministry in order to relieve her pain. As she proceeded to tell me the details of her story, she changed her mind; she wanted to know the truth. I explained to Ellie that I was glad she changed her mind because it would change her behavior. Her fatigue was connected to the all of the energy it took to suppress the flashbacks of extreme abuse.

I also wanted Ellie to understand that inner healing is not confined to the healing of emotions or restricted to truthful thoughts replacing lies. Inner healing is wholistic; it has an effect on the mind, body and spirit. Ellie began to realize that as God renews her mind, her emotions and her physical body will be transformed as well. Healing the scars of abuse begins in the mind, but it is not limited to the mind. It would take time, but she could experience complete health.

As Ellie's mind was renewed, her behavior did change. When I first met her, she was a recovering alcoholic. She now works with alcoholics and leads them into the path of recovery.

There is no formula that produces instant transformation. It is always a process. In the next chapter we will discuss various elements of health—mental, emotional, social and spiritual. We will begin with a crucial part of the recovery process for those whose lives have been fractured by abuse. This is the matter of forgiveness, and is a greatly misunderstood concept.

6

Forgiveness and Health

Forgiveness is a powerful Kingdom principle, and a vital step toward healing from abuse. Initially many survivors resist forgiving those who violated them because they believe that forgiveness means that the perpetrators will not be held accountable for the violent acts. This is not true. God is a perfect Judge, and those who abuse His children will have to face the consequences of their actions either in this world or the next.

People also tend to believe that forgiving their abusers excuses what they did. On the contrary, not forgiving their abusers actually allows their abusers to continue to have control over them. It keeps survivors from the freedom that God offers. By not forgiving their abusers they are actually going against the very thing that they desire, which is to be totally disconnected from them. People tell me that they did not realize this dynamic and agree that unforgiveness allows an unwanted connection to remain.

Survivors must choose forgiveness for the sake of their own hearts. Scripture is clear on this matter. Matthew 18:21–35 relates Jesus' words on this subject to His disciples.

Then Peter came and said to Him, "Lord, how often shall my brother sin against me and I forgive him? Up to seven times?" Jesus said to him, "I do not say to you, up to seven times, but up to seventy times seven.

"For this reason the kingdom of heaven may be compared to a king who wished to settle accounts with his slaves. When he had begun to settle them, one who owed him ten thousand talents was brought to him. But since he did not have the means to repay, his lord commanded him to be sold, along with his wife and children and all that he had, and repayment to be made. So the slave fell to the ground and prostrated himself before him, saying, 'Have patience with me and I will repay you everything.' And the lord of that slave felt compassion and released him and forgave him the debt. But that slave went out and found one of his fellow slaves who owed him a hundred denarii; and he seized him and began to choke him, saying, 'Pay back what you owe.' So his fellow slave fell to the ground and began to plead with him, saying, 'Have patience with me and I will repay you.' But he was unwilling and went and threw him in prison until he should pay back what was owed. So when his fellow slaves saw what had happened, they were deeply grieved and came and reported to their lord all that had happened. Then summoning him, his lord said to him, 'You wicked slave, I forgave you all that debt because you pleaded with me. Should you not also have had mercy on your fellow slave, in the same way that I had mercy on you?' And his lord, moved with anger, handed him over to the torturers until he should repay all that was owed him. My heavenly Father will also do the same to you, if each of you does not forgive his brother from your heart."

If survivors (or any of us who have been wronged) do not forgive from their hearts, their hearts will remain in prison. Our Father prefers mercy and not judgment (see James 2:13). Unforgiveness often is a form of judgment; it is the desire to see another pay for his sins. But the result is just the opposite: Judging others will result in our judgment (see Matthew 7:1–5). I once heard it said that unforgiveness is like drinking poison and waiting for the other person to die. Unforgiveness is poison to abuse survivors. They will never get well until they stop drinking that poison.

Survivors can choose to remove unforgiveness from their hearts. Lorrie, for instance, whose story we recounted in the last chapter, was traumatized by men who played worship music during their repeated violations of her. I asked Lorrie if she would be willing to forgive the men who raped her. Before she could answer me, I assured her that extending forgiveness to the men was not excusing their behavior. I wanted Lorrie to understand the powerful Kingdom principle of forgiveness on a personal level.

She listened as I told her that we should follow Jesus' example about dealing with people who hurt us. Jesus said we must forgive each other because the Father forgives us (see Ephesians 4:32). I also told her that Jesus said we should forgive all offenses that we have against each other (see Colossians 3:13). I suggested that Lorrie forgive her perpetrators and disconnect from any further ties that they had on her life. She agreed and was set free.

Scripture directs us to do for others what our Father has done for us. Jesus said in Luke 6:36, "Be merciful, just as your Father is merciful" (NIV). Our ability to forgive reveals the condition of our hearts. I repeat the principle of forgiveness every time a person expresses anger connected to an abuse memory.

I often share with survivors my desire to have a heart of love for Jesus like the woman whose story is told in Luke 7:36–50. Jesus liked her heart, and drew attention to the fact that, although she was not in a healed place, she demonstrated love that pleased Him. She was known as an immoral woman, yet she felt His unconditional love. All the religious men around that table despised her, but when she came up behind Jesus and anointed His feet with perfume and tears and wiped them with her hair, she felt love and acceptance from Him. That is why she was weeping. Before Jesus even pronounced her forgiven, she felt forgiven. Because she loved much, she was forgiven much. The greater our experience of forgiveness, the greater our love, and the greater our love, the greater our ability to forgive.

I agree readily with abuse survivors that they have been horribly violated, and that their abusers do not deserve forgiveness. But I encourage them to focus on their own hearts rather than the evil acts and evil hearts of the abusers. It is very important that prayer ministers do not drop into a "religious" attitude about forgiveness when ministering to survivors. A "just forgive and get over it" stance on our part can cause them to resist what we have to offer. The traumatized need our patience and mercy, not judgment. Years of abuse produce years of hopeless bitterness and anger. Forgiveness may come quickly, but more often it does not.

When individuals are not willing to forgive their abusers, I explain to them that they are allowing a barrier to remain in their hearts that will hinder their ability to be healed. I often suggest that we stop ministry for the day in order to allow them time to consider their choice to forgive. When unforgiveness becomes an issue for survivors, and they are stuck in a place where they refuse to forgive, I tell them to come back when they are ready to move forward.

Many brokenhearted people who have survived extreme abuse feel entitled to hold judgment and unforgiveness in their hearts. I stress the fact that we need to follow the example of Jesus and forgive. Forgiveness is an important part of healing and transformation. The choice to forgive or not to forgive, however, is their decision, and we cannot violate their choices.

Mental Health

When survivors agree with the importance of extending forgiveness and mercy, I begin to teach them about "health" and what it will look like in their lives. There is usually no grid for mental, emotional, social or spiritual health in the mind of an abuse survivor.

I start with what healthy thinking looks like. Romans 12:2 says: "Do not be conformed to this world, but be transformed by the renewing of your mind, so that you may prove what the will of God is, that which is good and acceptable and perfect." A renewed mind is a mind that can process thoughts appropriately. Behaviors cannot be separated from thoughts. Abuse survivors are usually amazed to hear that when their faulty thinking is replaced with truth, their thoughts will become healthy and they will be able to think clearly. This point often needs to be stressed: How they think is linked to how they behave and how they feel.

Change comes through thinking. Larry Crabb connects thinking, behaving and feeling when he says, "If I am to order my life correctly before God it is necessary to think correct thoughts. Wrong thinking leads to wrong behaving and feeling" (*Basic Principles of Biblical Counseling*, Zondervan, 1975). Healthy thinking is the ability to process daily life. It is the capacity to make good choices. It is the ability to make a decision without being afraid. A healthy person knows that what he is doing and what he is feeling stems from what he is thinking. Proverbs 23:7 says, "For as he thinks within himself, so he is." We are what we think.

Emotional Health

Trauma survivors are much more familiar with negative emotions than with positive emotions. They make decisions based on how afraid they are of something. Even though traumatized people are often very intelligent, their unhealthy emotions become their guide. This explains why smart, abused people often behave irrationally. It seems obvious, but many survivors have never considered that fear, paranoia, anxiety and many other negative emotions are not conducive to emotional health.

Intelligent people want to defend why they feel the way they do. Thus, they can present a logical case for being afraid. The response to this is to tell them that even though they are smart, they are wrong about believing it is all right to live in fear. God's peace—Emmanuel, God with us—should serve as our emotional barometer. Healthy, healed people do not live in fear; they live in peace. This is not to say that healthy people always feel peaceful, but they understand that when they do not feel peaceful something is going on in their hearts that they need to ask the Father about.

It is important for survivors of abuse to understand the role of emotions. Emotions indicate what we believe. Our emotions are often apparent long before our thoughts. It is common for survivors of abuse to tell me that they are afraid of some place, something or someone without understanding why. They are feeling what they believe.

Daniel Goleman uses the phrase *emotional intelligence* to describe this. I find this term helpful in addressing a person's awareness of his emotions. Goleman's definition of *emotional intelligence* is: abilities such as being able to motivate oneself and persist in the face of frustrations; to control impulse and delay gratification; to regulate one's moods and keep distress from swamping the ability to think; to empathize and to hope (*Emotional Intelligence*, Bantam, 1995).

A life of constant painful feelings makes a person weak and unable to experience many of these healthy benchmarks. I tell survivors that one of their inner healing goals is to restore their passions and longings. I want them to reconnect to the positive feelings that they knew outside of the world of abuse.

Healthy people are not limited to imbalanced feelings. Healthy people feel and express positive emotions. Healthy people can manage their emotions. They understand that strength comes from a joyful heart. They know that a happy heart is related to being strong and healthy. "Do not be grieved, for the joy of the LORD is your strength" (Nehemiah 8:10). Healthy emotions come from our Father.

Social Health

Emotionally healthy people are in relationship with others. Most of the abuse survivors that I have known prefer to live in isolation. I stress to those receiving prayer ministry that a noticeable sign of healing is the desire to engage in community. Socially intelligent people know how to interact with others. They can develop friendships based on the ability to relate in a healthy manner. Usually abuse survivors interact with others only in order to talk about their own pain. They lack the ability to care about the details of another person's life.

Goleman says that socially healthy people are able to empathize with other people's feelings by sensing non-verbal emotional signals; they are able to listen with full receptivity to another person; they understand another person's feelings and intentions; they know how the social world works (*Social Intelligence*, Bantam, 2006). Fragmented people have many social blind spots that hinder them from relating to others. Healthy people are social.

Spiritual Health

I describe spiritual health to survivors as the ability to stay intimately connected to God when circumstances in their lives feel overwhelming. Spiritually healthy individuals choose to turn to the Father to interpret bad things that happen. They avoid using people or objects to numb their pain. Healthy Christians know what helps them return to joy when their joy is disrupted. They know that the voice of God gives life (see John 6:63).

Survivors are seldom in touch with what makes them happy. I am frequently asked what I do when I am sad. I answer that the bathtub is my healing retreat. At the end of the day when I am troubled, I take a hot bath and ask God to tell me the truth that I need to know about the situation. Listening to worship music on a long walk is another act that makes my heart happy. I encourage people to find what restores joy for them. Many think that the only correct answer is to read the Bible. I remind them that healthy people do not feel religious restrictions, and that God speaks in many ways.

Healthy people choose to process pain with God and other trustworthy people. They know when God's voice is speaking to their hearts (see John 10:1–5). They trust Jesus. Freedom in Jesus allows a person in pain to know that nothing is too extreme for Him to heal: "For nothing will be impossible with God" (Luke 1:37).

Many survivors are afraid to process abuse memories because they fear that something bad will happen to them. Enduring many years of trauma has put them into a fearful state. Their fear will dissipate, however, as they realize that nothing bad will happen to them in our ministry time together. Healthy people are not afraid to remember the past, no matter what that past might be.

Survivors who forgive can have a good perspective on mental, emotional, social and spiritual health. Reconstructing their minds with truth will help them find that path to health.

7

Changing Your Mind— and Heart

Survivors usually grasp one important fact about renewal of their minds: Renewal takes place when their fragmented personalities hear and receive truth about the abuse.

This is accurate. It is, however, only one side of the equation. The other side is this: The person's conscious mind must, in turn, receive the truth that the fragmented personalities know.

So, on the one hand, the fragmented personalities need to know the "big picture" truth about the segment of abuse they have protected the core personality from knowing. A significant piece of wholeness occurs when the fragmented parts of a person share their secrets with each other.

On the other hand, the core personality must remember the things it has worked so diligently to forget. I refer to the things in a person's mind that we know about as *conscious awareness.* This side of inner healing ministry involves integrating what is hidden in the mind—the information held by the personalities—with the person's conscious awareness.

I simplify both sides of this equation by saying that the big person needs to know what the fragmented child parts know, and the fragmented child parts need to know what the big person knows. In addition, every part of the person needs to hear truth from Jesus. John 8:32 records these words of Jesus: "You will know the truth, and the truth will make you free." All of the fragmented parts of an abuse survivor need to know that the abuse was not their fault and that they are not like those who abused them. This truth must come from God.

Unless this exchange of truth takes place, these wounded individuals will remain in denial. If the big person hears truth about the abuse but the fragmented child parts still believe lies, the lies still have power. And if the parts receive the truth but the big person does not accept it, healing cannot come.

This principle of lies having power applies to everyone; it is not restricted to a divided mind. I am not an abuse survivor, for instance, and I do not have a divided mind, but if I believe a lie it can control me even if I am not aware of the lie.

Let's use this example. I believe that God will always take care of me because I know that the Bible tells me so (see Philippians 4:19). But suppose that every time I face a trial in my life I become anxious and function in opposition to my Bible knowledge. This means that there is a lie that I believe somewhere in my mind. Even if I am not aware of the lie, where it originated or how old I was when I first believed it, I will still respond to trials based on the hidden lie that I believe.

In order to resolve the power that the lie has over my thoughts, my emotions and my behaviors I need the Father to expose the root of the lie. I need Him to tell me the truth in the place where the lie is hidden. I must embrace God's truth in the present to change my future experience. Fragmented people want to compartmentalize truth. We help them see the importance of knowing the truth in every part of the mind.

Annie: Receiving Truth in All the Parts

Annie was a survivor of ritual abuse who had many fragmented child personalities. She thought everyone had fragmented personalities. She thought multiple conversations and arguments within the mind were normal. She acted surprised when I told her that I did not hear voices, conversations or arguments in my head.

As Annie began to tell the details that she knew about her story, many of the young personalities interrupted her to talk to me. Annie was unaware of the personalities' ability to do this. The personalities would come forward to contradict many of the details that Annie shared.

When I asked why she had come for prayer, Annie said that she wanted me to help her understand why a stranger was following her. Her voice softened to a whisper as she described a woman that she was afraid of. She told me how the woman would say strange things to her whenever their paths crossed in town. The comments were random and did not make sense, but she felt fear inside every time the woman spoke to her. Annie could not remember officially meeting this woman or give any reason why the woman should talk to her.

When I asked Annie to give me an example, she told me that the woman would pass her and grin in a scary manner and say, "Blue is the best color." The woman would also walk by her and wave a candy bar and say, "It's your favorite." Annie's voice changed to an even softer whisper as she told me that she was afraid that this woman was going to hurt her.

A child part interrupted Annie and said that Kay would never hurt anyone. I asked her who Kay was. "Kay is the lady that Annie is telling lies about. Kay is my friend. Kay knows my favorite color and my favorite candy. Every time that I go somewhere with Kay she gives me a treat. She is a nice lady."

I had many questions for the little girl, but I decided that the most valuable information was her name. "Do you have a name?" I asked.

"Yes, my name is Love, but Annie doesn't know me." I told Love that I would like to talk to her again later. She agreed. I asked if I could talk to Annie, but I was interrupted by an angry voice, yelling, "Love is a liar! Kay is a very bad person." This angry part of Annie began to tell me about the extreme ways in which Kay abused Annie. She screamed graphic details of physical, sexual and ritual abuse in which Kay was the perpetrator. She told me that during times of abuse she had to call Kay "The Queen," and added, "I know the truth about The Queen."

I assured the angry little girl that I was not like Kay. I told her that I believed her, that I was very sorry about what happened to her, and that I would like to help her. I assured her that I was not going to hurt her or trick her.

She began screaming again: "Annie and Love are the ones who need help, and they are stupid. One thinks Queen Kay is nice and the other one doesn't have a clue." Once again I told the little girl that I cared about her and every part of Annie and that I wanted to help her. She calmed down and said that she did not understand how I could help her. I told her about my friend Jesus and how He loves little children. She listened intently as I told her that Jesus could heal her. This part wanted me to call her the Bad One, but I asked her if I could call her Joy, and she agreed.

It took many months for Annie to acknowledge Love and Joy. It took more time for her to believe their experiences. Annie finally made a commitment to inner healing ministry, and she allowed me to pray and ask God to tell her the truth.

In the weeks that followed, she finally realized the truth about Kay and the abuse. She also realized that she needed to know the truth about every part of herself and what each had endured. She understood that all of her little girl parts needed to know the truth, and that they also needed to share their experiences with her. Annie believed that God was renewing her mind with truth, and she moved into wholeness as the division within her mind was healed.

Annie is no longer in denial about her childhood abuse. She no longer has a fragmented mind. Her story is a great example of the need for truth to be received in every recess of a fragmented mind, and also in the conscious awareness.

Maria: Facing Hard Facts

Initially, as we have seen, abuse survivors communicate their lives through the grid of denial. In John 8:32, Jesus' word for the *truth* that makes us free is *aletheia*, synonymous with the word *reality*. A significant aspect of a survivor's testimony is the fact that God's truth allows his mind to embrace reality. He no longer defines the past, present or future with a false mindset.

Reality for trauma survivors includes embracing the painful truth about their abuse and the ability to stop denying it or changing the memory of it. It is a wonderful experience to listen to a healed trauma survivor tell the truth about his past from a changed mind, without signs of pain and sorrow.

Maria had survived years of physical, sexual and spiritual abuse by those deemed as her caretakers. Although she remembered that her father was involved in her systematic occult abuse, she continued to make excuses for his incestuous behavior and minimize his involvement. Maria knew her father was involved, but she denied any evil intentions on his part. She tried to convince me that her father was a nice man who did not mean to hurt her.

Maria told me that sex was the only way her dad knew to communicate how much he loved her. She would always add, however, that she noticed changes in him whenever he sexually violated her. She said that his eyes looked different and that his voice did not sound like his voice when he was hurting her. She also could not understand why he would hit her violently if she cried when he was abusing her.

Maria was aware of the demonic activity that surrounded her father. She also knew that her father had molested her, but she was not willing to embrace the reality that he was responsible for his behavior. She blamed herself, concluding that she must have done something wrong.

I felt sad week after week to hear Maria create new excuses for her father's behavior and hold the little girl part of her responsible for the incest. I continued to ask the Holy Spirit to tell the little girl personality and Maria the truth. It appeared that it was easier for Maria to say that she was bad and deserved to be sexually abused than it was to admit her father's guilt. I continued to pray with and for Maria.

I remember the day when Maria realized the truth about her dad. I had prayed once again and asked the Holy Spirit to tell her the truth that she needed to know. She looked at me with great sadness through teary eyes and stated that she "realized" that her father knew what he was doing to her. She said that before she arrived at my office that day, she decided that it was time for the truth. She told me that Jesus made it very clear to her that her dad knew what he was doing.

I asked Maria if she felt that there was any other truth she needed to know. She sadly responded, "No, that's it." She continued to tell me that she felt as though this was a significant breakthrough for her. She confirmed my assumption about blaming herself and told me, "I know this sounds stupid, but it was easier for me to blame myself than to entertain the thought that my dad chose to abuse me."

It was as if the Holy Spirit turned on the lights in Maria's mind that day as she pronounced one truth after the next loudly in my office. Every time some aspect of her abuse made sense to her, she would blurt it out. She told me that she understood how occult involvement was an opening to demonic activity in her father's life. She told me she was relieved because Jesus said that she was not crazy.

Maria now tells her story from a perspective of truth and reality. It is a wonderful testimony of a survivor of extreme occult abuse telling others about how much Jesus loves her.

Maria and I continue to meet for times of prayer. She remembers the abuse memories with her father from a renewed perspective. She remembers them without the stain of lies and denial. She can now tell the truth about her life with a renewed mind.

Deciding to Trust God

The key to a renewed mind—and a transformed life—is a surrendered heart. Trauma leaves people with a self-sufficient mindset that limits their ability to receive healing from God. When a traumatized person is living life in survival mode, his trust is not in the Father. We need to encourage people who are trapped in pain to surrender their hearts to God. Brokenhearted people can learn not to trust their perspectives of what happened to them, but, rather, to trust God's truth.

I often remind people I pray with that Proverbs 3:5–6 tells us how to proceed: "Trust in the Lord with all your heart and do not lean on your own understanding. In all your ways acknowledge Him, and He will make your paths straight." This assures us that God will direct their healing journeys if they will choose to place their trust in Him. A surrendered heart means trusting God to heal the scars of abuse.

Even though survivors begin their journeys in denial and unaware of many details, their physical posture tells me that they are in emotional pain. Our body language communicates what our hearts are feeling. Our posture usually correlates with our emotions. A person who is happy will stand tall and straight. A depressed person who is full of shame will often walk and talk with head bowed. It fascinates me how often abuse survivors walk into my office slumped over with hats hiding their faces. They usually begin telling me their stories without looking at me, their heads hung low, eyes toward the floor. It reflects their weariness in the long battle to surrender their hearts and choose to trust God. It took Maria a long time to open her heart and listen to Jesus tell her the truth about her father.

In Psalm 4 David shows a great example of a surrendered heart and how it led him to trust God. David knew that the heavenly Father would answer him when he prayed: "But know that the LORD has set apart the godly man for Himself; the LORD hears when I call to Him" (verse 3). David's emotions matched his trust in God. He realized that his joy came from the Father: "You have put gladness in my heart" (verse 7). He experienced God's peace whether he was awake or asleep: "In peace I will both lie down and sleep" (verse 8).

This is comforting for a person who has been tormented for years with flashbacks or terrifying nightmares. They tell me that they would love to have a peaceful night's sleep. They like this Scripture. David's physical posture of lifting his head (see Psalm 3:3) and the posture of his heart in trusting the Father (see Psalm 4:5) can be used to encourage survivors who are stuck in a posture of survival. The trust with which a survivor and all his or her parts receive the truth comes from a surrendered heart.

Hearts—Surrendered and Not

A surrendered heart accelerates the healing process; a heart that is closed and resistant to the voice of God can be a hindrance to the healing process. I prayed with two individuals with opposite heart postures who exhibited this. Ben had an open heart and mind. Nick did not.

Ben and Nick bore the scars of long-term incest abuse. They had both been sexually violated in their homes by their parents. I learned that both young men had similar stories that confirmed generations of family trauma.

Ben was introduced to inner healing prayer ministry through a conference at his church. He felt certain that prayer ministry was the answer for his bondage. Since his church did not minister inner healing to what he called "difficult cases," he searched for someone who did. I had ministered to an abuse survivor in Ben's church who had received freedom in our prayer time together. That individual shared my contact information with Ben.

The first hour I spent with Ben I knew that he loved and trusted Jesus. I explained my approach to inner healing. I told him I believed that all scars of trauma could be healed through the work of the Holy Spirit, and he agreed. Ben showed many aspects of a surrendered heart: He was connected with the spiritual community in his church; he was a worshiper; he understood the Kingdom principle of truth replacing lies. Most important, he trusted Jesus to set him free.

Ben began by telling me that he did not know the truth about himself. He felt as though the incest had stolen his identity. Ben had childlike faith but he was bound by lies that he believed about himself. Because he felt disqualified to move forward in ministry, he had turned down numerous opportunities to lead worship and record his music.

I spent three days praying for Ben and asking Jesus to tell him the truth about himself. Ben's openness to hearing the voice of God made our ministry sessions easy. Jesus told Ben many truths about himself. Jesus assured Ben that he was well equipped to move forward in his music desires. By the end of our prayer time, Ben told me that he no longer believed the lies that he had once believed about himself. He was ready to receive the good things that the Father had for him. Ben is an example of approaching the Father with childlike faith and the release that can bring.

I wondered why Nick came to see me, because he argued with everything I said. He challenged the process of inner healing. He doubted that he could be free. He continually reframed the sexual abuse by his father and downplayed the effect of the abuse on his mind. He tried to convince me that abuse is "no big deal." Nick belonged to Jesus and he trusted Jesus to heal other people, but when it came to him, he was not teachable.

Nick was not willing to forgive his father. Although Nick disregarded his abuse scars, he told me emphatically that he would never forgive his father. He declared angrily that his father was the one who needed to ask for forgiveness.

I could not penetrate Nick's defensive heart posture. The condition of Nick's heart was blocking his ability to hear God's truth.

Nick continued to deny the significance of his abuse, which hindered the healing work of Jesus in his life. I told Nick that I did not think I could help him. I told him he was acting like a stubborn little child who was trying to get his own way. Because Nick's heart was closed and guarded, he left my office with the same abuse scars that he had entered with. Plus, he remained confused about the effects of abuse, inner healing and his true identity.

Ben came to Jesus with the heart attitude that allowed him to receive the truth about his identity. Ben welcomed his new life without the wounds of the past. He continues to grow relationally in community life in his home church. He continues to worship God. He continues to trust Jesus with everything in his life, but now he knows the truth about who he is.

Tom's Worshiping Heart

Tom, a survivor of incest, exhibited surrender and trust in his mind and heart. Tom loved Jesus. He trusted the Father in his daily life as well as during our times of ministry. When I met Tom his posture and his emotions conveyed a happy person. He had strong physical stature, and he smiled a lot and talked about loving God. He was a worship leader who acted as though his worship truly extended into his life.

Tom had come for prayer because he still felt tied to the past and did not understand why. Tom knew that he had been abused as a child; he grew up very aware of the scars of his abuse. He told me that he had received many hours of inner healing ministry, and he felt confident that he did not have dissociated or hidden abuse memories. Tom assured me that he was not in denial about his abuse: He knew that his father had sexually abused him; he remembered when the abuse started with his father; he remembered when it ended. He assured me that he was not resisting God's truth. So why, he wondered, was he still not fully free?

I asked Tom's permission to pray for him, which he agreed to readily. I told Tom that I was going to keep my prayer simple and ask Jesus to tell him the truth about his feelings of being tied to his past. My prayer was short: "Jesus, what's the truth that Tom needs to know?"

Tom looked at me calmly. "That makes sense," he said after a few moments. Tom then proceeded to tell me that Jesus had revealed to him that he had been abused by other people. Tom said that in his mind he had limited his abuse to his father.

I asked Tom if he was willing to allow the Holy Spirit to help him remember the abuse from other people. Tom's answer made me laugh. His answered confirmed his strong heart posture: "I don't care if the whole town abused me," he said. "I know Jesus will tell me the truth just as He did about my father. Pray for me."

Jesus told Tom that the abuse was not his fault. Before I could make the suggestion, Tom realized that he needed to forgive all of his abusers. Tom even asked Jesus if He would bless the abusers and provide a way for them to be healed. Tom then wanted me to ask Jesus to break anything that was tying him to the perpetrators. He was set free.

The Power of Truth in Making Changes

The testimony of a healed survivor is a powerful story. As with Annie, Maria, Ben and Tom, it is a story that encourages others who are trapped in the darkness of trauma to trust in the healing power of the Lord Jesus. A story told by a transformed abuse survivor is full of joy.

I like to talk to survivors about the importance of their testimonies and help them see what Revelation 12:11 means for them: "And they overcame [Satan] because of the blood of the Lamb and because of the word of their testimony." The "blood of the Lamb" refers to the sacrifice Jesus made for us and the healing that He made possible for all who say yes to it. This includes all of the mental, emotional, spiritual and physical scars of abuse. A testimony is the personal experience, the story, of overcoming the pain and dysfunction caused by the abuse. The survivor who opens his heart and mind to Jesus on his inner healing journey has a powerful testimony.

Revelation 12:11 further teaches survivors that their testimonies defeat Satan's schemes to keep them trapped in the bondage of deception. They can begin to realize the power that their stories hold as they experience new levels of freedom through Jesus. The power of their testimony is not restricted to overcoming the evils of their past; it also includes their future. When Satan torments them with the lie that their future is defined by their broken past, they can stand in the confidence that they know the truth, and that the truth has set them free.

Transformation begins with a renewed mind. This change is activated when the survivor decides to surrender his heart to the Father. This is, as I have mentioned, a challenging dynamic for prayer ministers, because we want to encourage abuse survivors to move forward in their healing, but we are confined to their personal choices. We are anxious to see a person healed, but we understand, on the other hand, that if they are not ready, their hearts will not be positioned to receive God's healing and they will merely be trying to please us.

For those who are afraid to trust the Father with things that are still hidden in their minds, we can pray that the Father will encourage them:

May our Lord Jesus Christ Himself and God our Father, who has loved us and given us eternal comfort and good hope by grace, comfort and strengthen your hearts in every good work and word.

2 Thessalonians 2:16–17

8

Let the Little Children Come to Him

It was story time, and the kindergartners were gathered at my feet anticipating a new adventure through a colorful book. This was my favorite time of the school day. The children loved stories. Their hearts connected to the emotions of the characters within the tale as their minds soaked up new information. It was easy to hold their attention. The children would often blurt out private family details that they believed enhanced the story. They had not yet learned what was acceptable to share in public and what should be kept private. They were transparent.

Jesus welcomed little children to come to Him. As I fondly remember my days of teaching preschool and kindergarten, I imagine Jesus with children sitting around His feet listening to His stories about the Kingdom. Jesus explained that it is easier for children to receive from Him than adults: "Whoever does not receive the kingdom of God like a child shall not enter at all" (Mark 10:15).

Jesus sees something in the heart of a child that He wants to bless. "And He took them in His arms and began blessing them, laying His hands upon them" (Mark 10:16).

Praying for Children

I love prayer ministry with little children. It is often very simple. I remember when Robert's parents brought him to pray with me. Robert, who was six years old, was having nightmares. He told me that when he closed his eyes monsters came into his brain and scared him.

I asked Robert if he wanted the monsters to go away. I explained to Robert that Jesus did not want the monsters to keep him awake. He assured me that Jesus was his friend, so I asked if I could pray for him. I first asked Robert to close his eyes to keep him from commenting on all of the pictures in my office. Then I prayed and asked Jesus what He wanted Robert to know about the monsters in his brain.

Robert blurted loudly, "Cool!"

Robert told me that Jesus came into his brain and destroyed the monsters for him. I love how Jesus speaks the truth in a way that even a little child can receive. Robert said that he was okay now, and that he could go home. He jumped up and headed for the door. I thought we should pray longer, but decided against it. His parents were waiting outside of my office. I asked them to let me know if his sleep improved.

They called me a week later to tell me that he did not have any more nightmares. The monsters were gone.

I did not have to give Robert's six-year-old mind a theological explanation. I did not have to quote chapter and verse of the Bible to assure him that nothing weird happened. I did not have to tell him my educational credentials. He had a child's heart that was receptive to the Kingdom of God. I think this is why Jesus says that He wants us to enter the Kingdom as a child.

I often pray with children who see, hear and experience Jesus effortlessly. It is so precious to witness children connecting with the Father. They often say to me, "Jesus is right here. Don't you see Him?" If I say no, they ask me what is wrong with me. Children are usually not bound by religion. Their hearts are open to the supernatural.

One of my precious little granddaughters was a toddler in her car seat one day when she looked upward and smiled, nodded her head and said, "Okay, pray for daddy." She raised her little hands, closed her eyes and said, "Jesus, Daddy!" This same granddaughter, a few years later, could see angels and report what she saw them doing in our home. Try asking many adults who have walked with Jesus for years if they are open to the spiritual reality of angels! Jesus wants us to approach Him with the heart of a child.

Going Deeper

Bonnie was five years old when her grandparents rescued her from satanic ritual abuse. When Bonnie visited her grandparents, she told them bizarre stories involving torture of people and animals and sexual violation. At first they thought the terrible stories were images from the horror movies Bonnie's parents watched in front of her. But as the stories became more and more graphic and disturbing, they realized that the child was in great danger and began the pursuit of custody. During that time, Bonnie's grandparents were granted permission to keep her for a few months while the parents traveled. They brought Bonnie to me for prayer.

Bonnie was not comfortable sitting on the couch across from me in my office and telling me her story. She said that she could not tell me about the bad stuff and look at me. I suggested that we draw pictures.

Bonnie sat on the floor in front of the couch in my office with a giant drawing pad and markers. She used only the black and red ones. She drew detailed abuse scenes and knew the perpetrators by name. Her drawings included dead animals, other children, many people who were tied with ropes and fire. She could describe the reason for the blood that was dripping from each person in her drawings.

When I asked Bonnie who the little girls were in the pictures, she answered, "They are both me. One had to go through the bad stuff and one of me didn't." Bonnie knew about her trauma, but she was disconnected from her feelings.

As I asked Bonnie about herself, she continued to draw, always looking down. She casually said that she was *gross* and *bad*. She told me, "I am just like the people in the woods."

I asked her what that meant.

"I am bad like them," she said. "They told me that."

I asked Bonnie if I could pray for her. She told me that it does not do any good to pray for bad girls. I suggested that she continue drawing while I prayed for her. I prayed and asked Jesus to tell her the truth.

After a few moments I asked her if Jesus told her anything. "He said the people in the woods lied to me. He said that I am not a bad girl." I continued to pray for Bonnie for the next few hours. She continued to draw. We ended our day by asking Jesus for a plan for Bonnie to get better. She did not like being afraid of so many things.

The following day Bonnie's pictures began to change. She still drew the pictures with animals, blood, fire and ropes, but she was no longer part of the pictures. The two little girls were drawn off to one side of the "bad stuff" in her drawings. Bonnie explained that Jesus took "both of her" out of the bad stuff. As Bonnie continued to draw she would occasionally act surprised by what she drew. When I asked her why she was surprised, she said that she did not recognize what the other part of her drew. She scrunched up her nose and looked at me and said, "She is me, too." She now felt safe looking at me.

This was the beginning of a little girl's healing journey with Jesus. On our last day together Bonnie reminded me that we needed a plan. She did not want to have to go back to the bad people.

I informed her grandparents about the content of the pictures and how Jesus spoke to Bonnie's heart while she drew pictures of her abuse memories. The grandparents and I prayed and asked the Father for wisdom about how to keep Bonnie safe until they received custody.

We felt the Holy Spirit's leading as we agreed that the grandparents needed to continue inner healing prayer with Bonnie at home. They became trained in inner healing prayer ministry and continued to pray for Bonnie and lead her closer to the Father.

Bonnie's grandparents were granted permanent custody. I speak with them every couple of years to hear how Bonnie is doing. She has overcome many of her fears. She knows the truth about her past and herself. She is familiar with the healing work of Jesus. Her healing journey began as a little girl who had a heart that was open to Jesus. Her journey continues with a heart that is receptive to the Holy Spirit.

Let me add here an important word for the lay prayer minister about reporting child abuse. If you are offering prayer ministry under the auspices of a church or private ministry, be sure that you are up-to-date on that service's guidelines for child safety. You might be required to notify the appropriate legal authorities.

As part of my initial paperwork with a new client, I include a "hold harmless clause," which states the fact that if a child shares with me that he or she is currently being abused, I am obligated by Kentucky law to report the situation to child protective services. I have done this on several occasions. There have been instances when I have insisted that the caretakers make the call from my office while I listen.

Do not think that prayer ministry excuses anyone from the law. Everyone has a responsibility to be aware of child abuse, whether that person is a licensed psychotherapist or church volunteer.

Talking to Child Personalities in Adults

I talk to fragmented child personalities within a person's mind the same way that I talk to little children in my office. When child personalities manifest I ask them to tell me their stories. Many times child personalities will say the same things to me that Bonnie said to me. They will tell me that they cannot look at me and tell me about the bad things that people did to them. In that case I often suggest that they draw.

I pray according to the traumatic story that each personality shares with me, applying the same procedure that I did with Bonnie. I ask the personalities if I can pray for them. I tell them about Jesus and how He always tells us the truth. I pray and ask Jesus to tell the personality the truth that he or she needs to know. Jesus is faithful to release truth to the part of the person's mind that is in need. I continue this process with each child personality that manifests. I help them embrace the inner healing principle that Holy Spirit truth will release them from every abuse memory that holds them hostage.

Many dissociated people who experience conflicting or confusing thoughts say that the voices in their minds resemble children arguing. I interact with these child personalities the same way I interact with children in a classroom. This is an effective tool.

I ask all of the children within the person's mind to sit down and agree to take turns talking. I then ask them if they know Jesus. If the personalities are familiar with Jesus, I ask if I can pray for them. I pray and ask Jesus to show the children where He is (in the person's mind). If they tell me that they see Jesus, I encourage them to stay close to Him.

This is not always easy because many of the child personalities might not trust Jesus and are not ready to get close to Him. I assure them that this is okay. I want them to choose to get close to Jesus, not do it because they think I want them to. I continue to encourage all of the child personalities who trust Jesus to stay close to Him until it is their turn to tell their stories. If personalities do not want anything to do with Jesus, I tell them that they may talk only when it is their turn.

When survivors welcome the truth about the child personalities within their minds, I suggest that they interact with the parts in a way that contributes to wholeness. I recommend that they begin to talk to their personalities—talking to the child personalities in the same way that I talk to them. This helps the individuals move in the direction of accepting every part of themselves.

People often disregard the importance of the ages of the personalities and the details they know about the abuse. The stories told by their fractured parts, however, are vital: They signify the personal abuse. Thus, I encourage every survivor to accept the fragmented child personalities, listen to what they have to say and understand that Jesus loves them and wants to heal them.

Coming with Childlike Faith

Crissy was confused about who she was. The many personalities within her mind added to her confusion.

When I met Crissy she had recently been released from a psychiatric hospital where she had been admitted for suicidal threats. Crissy was so confused she wanted to die. When I asked her why she came to see me, she told me that she wanted help, and that someone had told her that I would be nice to her and help her with healing and deliverance.

Crissy believed that demonic spirits were responsible for the annoying conversations that she could not silence in her mind. Although Crissy was extremely confused about who she was, she told me that she knew Jesus was the answer. She did not want to medicate her internal confusion; she did not want someone to help her analyze it; she did not want to learn skills to manage her pain. She wanted Jesus to heal her.

As Crissy continued to talk about her perspective on Jesus and healing, it became clear to me that she had child-like faith that would set the boundaries for her healing journey. In addition, Crissy was serious about healing: She moved to the town where I live so we could pray together on a regular basis.

I began by asking Crissy if she was familiar with the voice of God. She said no, but that she was willing to listen to Jesus. She liked the concept I explained to her about Jesus telling her the truth and the truth setting her free (see John 8:32).

Crissy was confused about demon possession, presuming that the voices she heard were demons talking in her mind. As we talked further, she told me that she believed that she was evil, full of demons, and needed me to make them go away.

I kept my response very simple. I told Crissy that because she belonged to Jesus, she could not be taken over or "possessed" by a demonic spirit. I helped her understand that as a Christian believer, she had authority over all demonic spirits. She was surprised but liked this truth and asked for scriptural verification.

I paraphrased Luke 10:17–20 and Mark 16:17, telling her that our authority is in the name of Jesus. I explained that when we tell demonic spirits to leave us alone in the name of Jesus, they must do so unless they have been given a right to continue to influence us. When we believe lies, for instance, we give demons certain "rights" to influence us. This happens because God is truth and no lies are connected to Him.

I suggested to Crissy that there might be another explanation for the conversations that she heard in her mind. I then explained about trauma and a fractured soul—and the fact that fragmented parts of a person cannot be prayed or commanded away. Crissy's childlike faith in Jesus led her to suggest that we find out if she was fragmented because of something bad happening to her. It made her sad to think about trying to get rid of part of herself.

Crissy and I prayed together for almost two years. Jesus helped her to remember that she had been abused her entire life. She realized that the voices in her mind were fragmented little girl personalities that helped her survive the years of abuse.

Crissy came to understand not only that demonic spirits did not fragment her mind, but also how to deal with any demonic spirits that tormented her. She and her child personalities learned about the authority that they had in the name of Jesus. After Jesus told them the truth about certain lies that they had believed, they would simply tell the demonic spirits attached to the lies to go away.

It was amazing to watch Crissy's healing journey. Regardless of painful details about her abuse or the sadness of remembering that family members took part in her abuse, Crissy always chose to ask Jesus to tell her the truth.

Jesus has healed Crissy's fragmented mind and healed her confusion. She now knows who she is, what she likes, and how to use her gifts and talents. Crissy told me that her friendship with Jesus is closer than it has ever been.

Crissy and I talk often. She tells me that she is doing great. She is in full-time ministry helping others understand how Jesus heals the scars of abuse. She has experienced personally the power of God's truth and can relate to the various stages of confusion within another person's journey.

The Question of Demonic Voices

Crissy's story is a good example of the way unhealed pain from abuse can make someone feel as though she is possessed by demons. It is not unusual for someone who hears "voices" in her head, particularly when those voices are arguing with one another, to be concerned that demons are controlling her.

You can assure survivors that when we belong to Jesus, we cannot be possessed by demonic spirits. This does not mean, however, that we are free from their taunts. Demonic spirits are opportunistic, and they will do everything possible to take advantage of the lies that trauma provides. They will try, for instance, to convince survivors that a person who has been through trauma is no different from her abusers. It is generally comforting for survivors to learn otherwise.

Survivors relax when they realize that they have authority over demonic spirits, even if their minds are fractured. In fact, in the name of Jesus every fragmented part has authority over demonic spirits. Survivors can usually discern the difference between angry fragmented personalities and demonic spirits.

Many Christians, not just survivors, are confused about deliverance from demonic oppression. They want to make it complicated and dramatic. I tell people that the easiest way to be released from demonic oppression is to ask God to expose the lies that they believe. Sometimes I have a sense that demonic spirits are successful in tormenting people because those individuals do not understand the significance of lies. After all, Satan is called the father of lies (see John 8:44).

We can help abuse survivors with fractured minds understand the relationships between trauma, lies and demonic oppression. Most people who have survived extreme abuse as children have believed numerous lies. Many survivors tell me that they have been tormented by demonic spirits for years. It brings great freedom for them to realize that the lies they have believed are the opening for demonic harassment—it lessens the fear that they themselves are evil.

Lies create opportunities for demonic torment, whether we have an abuse history or not. When God tells us the truth and we believe it, demonic spirits lose their right to harass us in that area.

I teach fractured people that they have authority over demonic spirits, but that angry, hurting parts of themselves cannot be sent away as if they were demonic spirits. Prayer can distinguish between the two. I demonstrate this by praying for those who are confused about the origin of the voices in their mind. My prayer is simple.

I begin by assuring the person that I do not believe that any part of them is evil—even if there are parts inside that believe they are evil or believe that they are a demon. I explain that when little children are physically or sexually violated they often believe that they are bad and dirty, but that I do not believe that. I pray and say, "In the name of Jesus I take authority over any demonic spirit that is harassing any part of this person. I command you to separate from any part of their humanity and go to the feet of Jesus."

Then I ask the survivor if she still hears the voices. If she says yes, I tell her that she is probably hearing a fragmented child part. I ask if I can talk to the voice that she is hearing. This usually confirms that the voice is a fragmented personality.

Sometimes when I pray and take authority, the voices that the person hears stop. This tells me that the voices were demonic spirits. In this situation I explain to the person that it is wise to ask the Father to reveal the reason why they were hearing a demonic spirit. This prayer usually reveals a lie that the person believes, so we ask God for truth. I suggest that the person tell the demonic spirit to leave her alone in the name of Jesus. This builds a person's experiential awareness of freedom from darkness. It also transitions a person from ignorance about the demonic to the reality of healing and deliverance.

It is easier for us to receive healing and deliverance from our Father if our hearts are accessible like the heart of a child. This is a position that carries great authority in the spiritual realm. When Jesus blesses our childlike faith, it leads to wholeness and welcomes the Kingdom of God into our midst: "But Jesus said, 'Let the children alone, and do not hinder them from coming to Me; for the kingdom of heaven belongs to such as these'" (Matthew 19:14).

9

Life after Wholeness

I am afraid I won't be able to function without my personalities. They have helped me for so many years!"
   After coming to Jesus for the truth about her traumatic childhood, Karen was ready to walk in wholeness. The fragmented personalities within her mind had been integrated. But now she had a new problem. Her personalities were no longer available to perform tasks that she was afraid to do. Until this time it had been normal, for instance, for Karen to step aside and allow a self-assured part of herself to interact with men that she feared, or to perform certain tasks at work with confidence. Now Karen felt alone. She was afraid of wholeness.

Missing the Personalities

Karen's concern was not unusual. This might sound bizarre, but traumatized people often experience deep sadness when they realize they will no longer be relying on personalities within their minds. They desire complete healing and wholeness, but the thought of losing something so familiar is painful.

This is usually because survivors have a false perception of what mental wholeness means. They typically believe that the fragmented parts of themselves are going to die. Prayer ministers can be quick to clarify: None of the personalities will die; none is being sent away. The fractured parts will be embraced and will function just as they did before trauma divided them. One survivor in my office explained it this way to another survivor: "It's as though everybody is out at the same time forever. Everybody becomes the same person."

Along with concern for the fate of their personalities, survivors also have a distorted view of what they will become after their minds are healed. Their expectations are often idealistic and disconnected from a true perspective of their original, core personality, giftedness and emotional health.

Abuse survivors who have had multiple personalities since childhood need prayer ministers to help them understand what life will be like for them as single-minded persons. We fall short of ministering to highly traumatized people if we do not provide a realistic goal for them following the process of integration. That will be the focus of these next three chapters.

I define *integration* as, first, the joining of all of the now-healed fragmented parts of a person with each other and with the core or true self, and, second, the challenge of learning to function without them. This process occurs naturally when the person is no longer in denial and feels safe enough to stop hiding things. Abuse survivors who know the truth about their traumatic histories realize eventually that they do not need fragmented parts to protect themselves. They walk in wholeness when they realize that Jesus is the only one who can show them truth in every situation they will face, and they rely on Him.

When survivors tell me that they are afraid they will be lonely or unable to function without their personalities, I ask if I can pray for them. I then pray and ask Jesus if He would tell them the truth about being alone. I also pray and ask the Father if He would fill the void inside of these persons with Himself.

On a practical note, before a person's mind is healed and whole, I encourage the person to tell the personalities that she appreciates how they helped her survive. She might want, further, to express to the personalities the fact that Jesus is going to keep them safe and continue to tell them the truth. Many survivors need time to say good-bye to their internal helpers before they embrace them into wholeness.

As I have mentioned, we also need to alert survivors to the fact that flashbacks often continue after wholeness occurs. There can be additional abuse memories that need to be processed. If a survivor does not understand this, she might doubt her healing. The process of receiving truth is the same after integration.

The Healing of the Body Comes Next

After survivors experience healing in their minds and begin to adjust to life without multiple personalities, I talk to them about their physical bodies. Pain can be stored in their bodies as well as their minds. As I mentioned in chapter 5, this experience is known as a *body memory*. It is as if the body remembers and reexperiences the trauma when the mind has separated from it. People will often come to me saying that they feel pressure in their chests or that their faces are numb. These people also tell me that their physicians have given them a clean bill of health.

When I hear this, I pray and ask the Holy Spirit what their bodies are feeling. It is very common, in the example of chest pain and numb faces, for instance, for the person to remember someone lying on top of them while pressing a hand over their mouths to keep them quiet. Prayer frequently confirms that what their bodies are feeling in the present is what they literally felt during times of trauma.

We should never tell someone we are praying with that we think she is feeling the effects of trauma, because that is directive. It is important that we allow the Holy Spirit to direct all aspects of inner healing ministry. Simply ask the person if you can pray for her and ask the Father to tell her the truth about what she is experiencing.

People frequently tell me that once they have broken out from denial, they begin to experience new levels of physical pain. I think that their bodies are releasing pain that was being disregarded due to their fractured minds. It is usual for people to feel pain in their bodies as they remember how they were violated. Many survivors feel physical pain during ministry times of processing abuse memories. We can pray and ask the Father to release this pain.

Many survivors have health issues that are related to pain trapped in their bodies. I have never prayed with a survivor of satanic ritual abuse that began in childhood who did not have health problems. Young children are often given mind-altering drugs during times of ritual abuse to distort the child's sense of reality. They are also often given large doses of antibiotics for extended periods of time that weaken the child's immune system. The antibiotics are intended to prevent disease that the child is exposed to with numerous sexual acts. The abuse of drugs combined with sexual and physical abuse weakens a child's natural response to fight sickness. The person is left with a compromised immune system that is in need of rebuilding.

Part of my ministry protocol for survivors of ritual abuse includes a homeopathic approach to improving their physical health. I often recommend the person visit a local physician who is familiar with the inner healing process and understands the benefits of a holistic approach to healing. I suggest that the survivor begin a schedule of healthy eating and exercise.

The allopathic medical community understands the relationship between long-term abuse and the effect it has on a person's well-being. Most medical professionals understand that stress often influences a person's state of health. We hear reports from the health community, for instance, that high blood pressure is related to a poor diet and unresolved stress. Health care providers also relate some forms of heart disease to the level of stress in the person's life.

Men and women who have survived years of abuse have emotional and physical scars that need to be addressed in the healing journey. I encourage abuse survivors to pursue a holistic approach to healing—by addressing the body, soul and spirit. I suggest that we expand our vision to include helping survivors understand the role their bodies play as well as their hearts and minds.

Emotional Healing

As survivors' minds are healed and their bodies gain health, their emotions also need to be addressed.

Abuse narrows the scope of a person's emotions. Traumatized people are acquainted with negative feelings but are unfamiliar with positive feelings. Plus, they are often trapped in emotions that accompany unwanted sexual feelings. Having spent so much time interpreting life through the lens of fear, they expect bad things to happen to them. Their feelings have been defined, interpreted and experienced though the abuse that robbed them for many years. In the beginning stages of wholeness people often need someone to process their emotions with. They need help discerning the appropriate emotion for a given situation.

A large component of wholeness is introducing survivors to the goodness of God. It is essential that we help them understand that all good things come from the Father, and this includes positive emotions. Teaching people who have known only fear and sadness the truth about joy, peace and contentment is quite a task. This part of the healing process also takes time.

And this is the reason why prayer ministers must be happy, content, peaceful people who get their strength from the Lord. This should be a natural part of our walk with the Father if we want to be successful in representing the joy of the Lord to the brokenhearted. Not only do we model healthy emotions for them, but we need to remain positive and peaceful during the long time it takes for them to learn to experience positive emotions. Positive emotions begin to replace negative emotions when a person is exposed to the good things of our Father.

We explain positive emotions in the context of the reality of negative emotions. Negative emotions are an appropriate response to many situations in life. Survivors, however, do not have the capacity to recover from negative emotions. They often get stuck in them because they have been so attached to them. We teach them to return to joy when normal bad things (I am not speaking here of traumatic abuse) happen to them. We help equip those who are entering a state of wholeness with skills to live a healthy emotional life. Emotionally healthy people understand what they are feeling.

Karen has become proficient at evaluating her emotions. She has adjusted to a mind that is free from the voices of many personalities, and she is working on her physical health.

She likes to have someone to process life with. Although Karen and I no longer process her abuse memories together, we meet for coffee and conversation. She tells me that it is helpful when she can tell me about her life and hear about mine. She is growing in her ability to make wise decisions. She is in a deeper place of intimacy with the Father. She is working on receiving good things in her life. She knows that good things come from God, even though she has not learned how to embrace them yet. She wants to share her story, but she does not yet know how.

As we discuss further in the next chapter, survivors need to learn the skill of communicating their stories without relaying the horrific details. They realize the power of testimony, but they lack the ability to share it without traumatizing others with its content. Talking with them through this stage of healing is an important way to help people develop their ability to communicate.

Some Lost Abilities in Integration

Prayer ministers also need to be prepared to help survivors deal with the possible loss of some tasks in the process of growing in wholeness. They actually might not be able to do some of the things that the individual personalities could do. This might sound odd, but sometimes after mental and emotional wholeness occurs, some abilities can go away with the integration of personalities. I am not going to attempt an explanation; however, I have witnessed this situation in many people. I have seen abilities cease when the person's mind was made whole.

Melody had multiple personalities that were connected to surviving years of abuse. One of her personalities could play the piano. Melody told me that this particular personality was a concert pianist. She had played in numerous concerts since Melody was a little girl. Melody played the piano for me on one occasion, and it was easy to tell that she was a gifted musician.

After several years of inner healing ministry, many of Melody's personalities were integrated. It was amazing to watch her try to play the piano. She struggled to play elementary music. Melody's reality included the loss of musical ability when the fragmented little girl personality who played the piano was embraced into wholeness within her mind.

When I met Dawn, she could not perform basic life skills such as going to the grocery store alone or keeping track of small amounts of money. She had to be reminded to shower because her hair was dirty. She struggled to comprehend a lighthearted conversation. She gave every indication of being limited in her cognitive abilities.

As Dawn continued to tell me about her life, I learned that she had earned a master's degree in biology with a 4.0 average. But when I asked her some basic biology questions, she could not comprehend what I was talking about. I wondered about this until Dawn explained that she had a personality who went to school. Once she completed her educational goals, the "smart" personality was no longer needed. Dawn told me, "If I don't need a girl inside to do something for me, she becomes part of me."

Teresa was a highly functioning abuse survivor. She had earned several degrees, including a degree in theology, and was well-versed in the Scriptures. She was beautiful and confident. (I would say that she was overconfident). She was artistic. She was socially active. She was obviously a woman who could multitask.

Her ability to multitask ceased when Teresa was integrated. She could not remember anything. She was scattered—and happy. No longer able to function at her once impressive state of productivity, she now focused on only one task at a time. She did retain her familiarity with the Scriptures, but her approach to the Word changed. She acted as though she enjoyed her time reading the Bible and talking about it. She no longer preached "at" me with her biblical knowledge.

These three women experienced new levels of wholeness when the personalities within their minds were integrated. They gained freedom, but they lost some abilities.

I encourage prayer ministers not to become crippled by the things that we cannot explain. Inner healing is not a systematic science with a set of laws to be applied precisely. Inner healing is more like an art. It is the art of learning to follow the Holy Spirit as He ministers to specific needs within unique individuals. We need to discuss this potential aspect of wholeness as we help traumatized people understand what they might experience without a divided mind.

Keeping Your Balance

A balanced approach to ministry encourages survivors to consider developing their lives with God, devoting attention to exercise and nutrition, as well as cultivating friendships while they are pursuing inner healing. If we limit inner healing ministry to resolving abuse memories, then it becomes introspective and imbalanced. On the other hand, if we teach survivors only about the character of God and stress church or community involvement, they will become equally off-balance and continue hiding their abuse scars.

As prayer ministers we need to have a balanced approach when we minister to others and in our own personal journeys of transformation. If we keep our eyes on the Father and allow the Holy Spirit to direct us, we will be balanced. "I will instruct you and teach you in the way which you should go; I will counsel you with My eye upon you" (Psalm 32:8).

Providing survivors with an understanding of what to expect after the fragmented personalities within their minds are integrated is a healthy, holistic ministry approach. Healing the scars of abuse should include the ability to experience positive emotions. It should include openness to receiving the good things that the Father has to give. It should include the capacity to engage in Kingdom community in a healthy manner.

Let's learn more about helping survivors grow in Kingdom living.

10

Kingdom Life and Community for Survivors

Our church has several community groups that meet together weekly to worship, pray and learn to love each other. We value authentic fellowship and desire for it to become a regular part of people's lives. Our church believes that small, intimate groups should be a safe place where each person can discover who he or she is in Jesus. My husband and I lead a few of these groups.

JC is host for one of the home groups that my husband and I lead. We position ourselves around JC's living room so we can see each other, for we understand the importance of eye contact and body language. We desire transparency. We are committed to inviting the Holy Spirit to search our hearts, so we encourage specific prayers of inner healing for whoever feels led by God to receive ministry. We desire to become more like our heavenly Father. We have made a commitment to be vulnerable to each other as well as to the Holy Spirit.

Our group is inclusive. We enjoy the new faces that show up and we enjoy listening to each person's story. We listen for victory in everyone's testimony, but we also listen for pain. We want to be known as a place where people feel safe to expose their wounds so we can pray for their healing. I think we do a good job in this area.

Angie Shocks the Group

Because our group is open to all who want to join us, it is not unusual for someone in ministry with me to attend. Since our home group is open to having a highly traumatized, unhealed person join us, I felt free to invite Angie to JC's house. Nevertheless, while several of us were familiar with the scars of abuse and a broken person's inability to share her story appropriately, that could not be said of everyone.

I watched the wide eyes of many people in JC's living room the first night that Angie came. Angie was a satanic ritual abuse survivor. She had relocated to Kentucky so she could receive regular times of ministry from me. She was not integrated. She was socially challenged. Angie's words had no filter.

The stories of trauma survivors who are in the early stages of receiving inner healing ministry are always based on the scars of their abuse. Their stories leak the emotional pain that accompanies a life of devastation. Their stories also reveal their hope—or lack of it—for the present and the future. It tells listeners that these individuals have lost their identity and are looking for people or things to fill the emotional vacancies. Their stories are usually spoken in tones of sadness because their stories are sad.

Angie, like many unhealed survivors, gave unnecessary graphic details. I believe that everyone in the room felt compassion for her; I also believe, however, that many felt personally violated by the content that was spewed into the environment.

Angie created tension in the room. No one wanted to dishonor her by shutting down her need to share, but allowing her to continue was not fair to the others. I interrupted Angie and ask if we could talk privately in the kitchen. Once there, I told Angie that many people were unfamiliar with the details of ritual abuse—and it was fine to leave it that way. I told her that the only people who need to know the details of her abuse are the people who are part of her solution. Graphic details are not a requirement for prayer requests.

Angie became angry and insisted that I was trying to kick her out of our fellowship. The pain of unresolved abuse memories trapped inside her mind would not allow her to relate to others in a healthy manner. Angie returned to home group each week, but would not allow the same personality to be present twice. The next week a "religious" personality was presented to our group, followed by a seductive personality. We met many parts of Angie's fragmented mind during the next several months.

Although the people in the home group did not understand the complexity of Angie's behaviors, they continued to embrace her, even as she continued to find ways to draw attention to herself. Granted, some people in the fellowship were more comfortable with her than others. Angie and I continued to meet together and uncover the hidden things that she struggled to admit. She appeared to want healing. I thought she was committed to the inner healing process.

The more time I spent in prayer with Angie, however, the more I noticed that she was not. In particular, I saw a pattern developing. Angie was telling me the same memory in a different context over and over again. I made it clear that I would pray with her only if she told me the truth. If she wanted to deceive me, she could do so easily by telling me memories that were on the surface and refusing to acknowledge what the Holy Spirit revealed to her about the root cause of her abuse.

After this confrontation, Angie left and never came back to see me. I was bound by her choice. The people in our home group who had invested so much were bound by her choice. She chose not to trust.

Teachable Katie

Katie was a different story. A victim of incest with multiple personalities, she was learning to trust God to heal the scars. Katie moved to our area for ministry, and liked living in our small town and attending our weekly small group. Because she understood the process of inner healing and spent a lot of time reading the Bible, she often contributed positively to the discussions in JC's home. There were times, however, when she interrupted others and contradicted what they were sharing. The people in our home group, who were beginning to understand the behaviors of abuse survivors, related to her with kindness.

Katie's pain manifested differently from Angie's behavior in a social setting. Katie could be transparent without being offensive. She was committed to the hard work of the inner healing process. She was being transformed in many areas of her life.

Katie's abuse had left her in the same condition as many other abuse survivors, without socialization skills. But Katie was teachable—in fact, she knew she needed help. She realized the importance of community in the process of healing and transformation. As part of her growth toward wholeness, she gave me and a few other people in our community permission to help her learn to interact with others in a healthy way. We continued to pray together, and she attended our small group until we both agreed that it was time for her to return to her hometown.

Helping Free Survivors from Isolation

I believe that no one can become whole and healthy in isolation. We need each other in order to discover our true identity. This applies to everyone, not just those who have traumatic backgrounds. I realize that it is easier for some people to interact in a small group setting than others. Still, no one can ever become like Jesus unless he or she forms deep friendships. Good small groups are perfect for providing an environment that is conducive to forming those friendships.

Traumatized people are often drawn to living in isolation. They tell me that community does not feel safe to them. I understand that their view of "safe" groups of people has been tainted by abuse; many survivors have been violated by groups of people. Nonetheless, we should emphasize the importance of connecting with others. Isolation leads to introspection. Community promotes a heart of service.

Part of the healing journey for abuse survivors, as well as anyone who desires to grow in his spiritual life, includes interacting with safe, healthy, godly people. Because I understand survivors' resistance to group gatherings, I will offer to go with them to church or home group get-togethers. This gives them a sense of security. When we extend love to the brokenhearted, it often relieves some of their social fear. First John 4:18 tells us that there is no fear in love.

Setting Boundaries

I believe that ministering to hopeless people involves a willingness to invest in them and the ability to respect the process of the healing journey. Each person will progress at a different pace according to the many dynamics unique to that particular situation. An effective prayer minister is a person who is in sync with our Father, the Holy Spirit and Jesus.

Hopeless people do not just feel alone; they feel abandoned. They feel separated from God and others. They even feel separated from themselves. I make a commitment to those I minister to and assure them that I will not give up on them. It releases hope in them when they feel the assurance that someone is willing to spend time and energy in their healing.

While we can encourage social contact, however, we need to work within appropriate boundaries. Here are some guidelines for both the prayer minister and the person receiving prayer.

Boundaries for the Prayer Minister

One of the greatest comforts to a person who feels alone is company. People tell me that they appreciate knowing that I am willing to commit time and energy to them during their healing journeys. They feel safe having someone to help them process their thoughts and feelings in a casual setting outside the ministry time, with its difficult hours spent in the process of resolving painful memories. When people feel hopeful, they begin to believe that they can be healed and made whole. They are more comfortable with submitting to the process of renewing the mind.

Socializing together can be a wonderful aid to ministry, but there are important cautions to consider. Prayer ministers must have healthy boundaries with abuse survivors and the ability to enforce them. I set up boundaries during the first ministry session I have with a person. For starters, I tell traumatized people that I am a prayer minister and not a psychiatrist. I am not, for instance, qualified to treat threats of suicide. I explain clearly that if they tell me they are experiencing suicidal thoughts and feel as if they want to die, I will call the police or take them to the emergency room.

Abuse survivors are usually needy people. They do not understand why others set limits on the amount of time they are willing to devote to them. I find in my ministry that lonely, traumatized people feel entitled to my time. If I go to lunch with them, they expect me to go to dinner with them as well. If I pick them up for church and arrange for someone else to drive them home, they get mad because they assumed I would spend the day with them. I have had many survivors get angry with me because I would not let them call me at home at night unless it was an emergency. I define emergency as illness or intense suicidal thoughts.

Be on the watch for survivors to try to manipulate your time and attention. I have had several people try to manipulate me by calling to say they felt suicidal, and that if I did not come and pray with them immediately they would hurt themselves. I responded by saying that if they are suicidal they need to go to the emergency room at once, and that I am going to call the police and ask that an officer be dispatched to their homes as soon as possible.

When they realize the ploy did not work, I remind them that because I care about them I will always do what is best for them, and the best thing I can do for them if they want to hurt themselves is to seek medical intervention.

Decide what you are willing to do and what you are not willing to do, and stick to it. This is another reason why community is so important. We need people in our lives who will tell us if they see our boundaries slipping and our lives being manipulated. Listen to them.

Boundaries for the Survivor

As we maintain appropriate boundaries for ourselves, we also need to help set appropriate boundaries in group settings regarding those we minister to. In our home group setting, JC, my husband and I, and several others understand the importance of boundaries in protecting a person who wants to receive prayer, as well as those who are new to a group.

Let me state once again that specific details of abuse do not need to be shared in order to pray for a person in pain. We often restate this when we have visitors. We encourage survivors to feel free to tell the group if they have been traumatized, and that it is okay to tell the group if it was ritual, spiritual, sexual or physical abuse, but that names and details are inappropriate for a social group setting. If broken people need to talk to someone in a more detailed manner about their abuse, we explain that we can set up a ministry session through the "transformation center" at our church.

Many wounded people who join our group express appreciation that our church offers a place where they can share their painful histories with people who are trained to listen to God and pray for them. I am up-front in letting people know that I apply this principle to myself as well. I often ask for prayer during home group by sharing my request in a general manner. If I feel that I need to embrace specific details of an issue, I set up a private prayer session with one of my prayer partners. Prayer ministers need to be authentic in their inner healing journeys if they are advising others to do so.

I remember when Mac moved to our community to pursue inner healing ministry from me. I invited him to JC's home group, where he listened intently to the lesson on forgiveness. Then when the time came for prayer requests, Mac's attentive, cooperative demeanor changed. He began by saying that he was struggling to forgive the people who abused him. This made sense to those in the room. Several people nodded their heads as if they were relating to some level of unforgiveness in their own lives.

Then, in an angry tone, Mac began naming his abusers. I quickly interrupted Mac, asking him to step into the kitchen with me, and asked JC to continue prayer for the needs of the group.

Once in the privacy of the kitchen, Mac expressed his surprise at my actions. I began by restating to Mac what I had said at the beginning of the evening about appropriate and inappropriate sharing of details. At first Mac spoke angrily in his defense, but he calmed down when I reminded him that during our inner healing prayer sessions he would have sufficient time to talk about the details of his anger. He then thanked me and returned to the living room where he did not talk the rest of the meeting.

Prayer ministers in a group setting will likely run into situations like this. It is important to understand ministry boundaries for the wounded, and be ready to enforce them.

Be Prepared for Displaced Anger

I want to be honest about the difficulty of leading the traumatized out of bondage and into wholeness. It is not always easy. It is often painful. When children are violated at an early age, it interrupts their emotional development, which, among other things, stifles their social abilities. When abuse continues until adulthood, these individuals do not have the ability to interact in appropriate ways. Many times their anger is displaced and prayer ministers become their targets as they release years of denied emotions.

I have not worked with many trauma survivors who have not broken my heart. I have struggled to continue to minister to those who lack the ability to know the difference between those who hurt them and those who are trying to help them. Rachel is an example of a person in whom I invested months of my time and energy in prayer ministry and who expressed toxic feelings toward me.

After Rachael's mind was integrated, I spent many hours teaching her the truth about God. I tried to help her discern the difference between her abusive earthly father and our heavenly Father. She was welcomed into our church community and attended church home groups. Rachael was exerting effort and presented an attitude of a person who wanted to be healthy. The problem was, however, that Rachael had no social intelligence. She was not aware of the feelings of others. She was unable to tune in or acknowledge any conversation that was not about her. If Rachael could not direct conversations to focus on her, she "checked out."

Healthy individuals have the ability to listen to others, read their cues, make eye contact and respond with appropriate interest. They are not narcissistic, and they do not hijack conversations. They can engage in mutuality. Rachael could not. I tried to talk to her about her behavior, but she became angry. That marked the beginning of her attacks toward me.

Rachael began to accuse me of making up her abuse history. She told me that I was no different from the evil people from whom she had at one time wanted to disconnect. She told people in the community that our healing team was deceptive and wanted to destroy her. At that point she left our church community and our town and returned to the people she had originally identified as her perpetrators. Rachael's social anxiety was an opportunity for demonic spirits to bring division and end her inner healing journey. I was not defensive; I was heartbroken.

It was this painful experience with Rachael that led me in the direction of a holistic inner healing ministry approach. I learned firsthand from this sad scenario that a person's inner healing experience needs to be balanced. People should not put their lives on pause so that they can spend all of their time receiving ministry; they can learn to function in the world and still allow God to heal them.

Overcoming a traumatic history involves more than processing abuse memories; it includes post-integration work to learn skills that equip a survivor to know the will of the Father and interact with others appropriately. We need a balanced ministry model that will enable us to partner with the Father in leading traumatized people into wholeness. Otherwise, even if they integrate internally, they might remain isolated from a healthy community and never develop fully into all that the Father desires for them.

One More Hard Lesson

Let me tell you one more story about learning this hard lesson of the many ways that wounded people can displace their pain and anger toward those who try to help them. We must practice forgiveness and choose to continue to live in community, but we must be informed of the hazards.

Both young women began inner healing ministry with me at the same time. They were not related to each other, but had similar stories of abuse. Although their histories ran parallel, they were complete opposites in every other area of their lives. One of the young women was what I would describe as a high-maintenance female. She was very feminine and appearance-conscious. She was an artist who approached life with a creative flair. She was easy to like, and easy to embrace in community.

The other young woman was attractive, but she prided herself in being a tough girl and had traits that seemed masculine. She was well-traveled and adventurous. I would not have been surprised if she had told me she enjoyed the danger of extreme sports. Even though she had a pleasant personality, she was not easy to like. Still, I welcomed her into our community.

I invested several years of ministry with both women. In fact, I shared my life with them. They were welcomed into several small groups and had many opportunities to interact with other people in the church. They both appeared to be growing spiritually and socially. I felt confident that both of them trusted me. They said they did. Then they both manifested drastic behavioral changes toward me within the same month.

One of the women became angry and accused me of making up her abuse history, for she now knew uncategorically, she said, that she had never been abused. She told lies about me to everyone she came in contact with. She worked hard to convince people that I had hurt her, lied to her, was holding her hostage and forcing her to agree with my view on healing.

I was guilty of trusting her prematurely. I believed that she was further in her healing journey than she actually was. I thought she had matured in her ability to understand what she was feeling and to talk to me about it. In hindsight, it is obvious that she was still confused and afraid of moving forward in life. Dysfunctional, unhealthy relationships had become normal for her. She did not know how to relate to me in a healthy manner. We parted ways on negative terms.

The other woman suddenly decided that I was unqualified to minister to abuse survivors. She countered everything we had worked so long to establish.

Here are a few examples of the divergent track our sessions took. I encouraged her to spend time with healthy, healed people; she insisted that her friendships be with unhealed abuse survivors because they could relate to her better. I shared with her my belief that no one can become healthy and whole apart from other people, particularly people in a healthy spiritual community; she countered that it was a good idea to live life disconnected from people in order to seek God. I worked with her by following the leading of the Holy Spirit, believing that He will let survivors know what details are important for their freedom; she stressed the importance of uncovering specific details of her abuse on her own.

I made an effort to check on her status the following year, but she would not respond to me. To this day, I do not understand what triggered her drastic behavior change. I was very sad that this person disappeared. I cared about her and wanted to see her healed. She had her own agenda, however, and it did not include me. Nor did it include my approach to healing, deliverance or wholeness.

I was discouraged after working with these two women. I wanted to quit. I felt foolish for trusting risky people. I cried a lot. I entertained the thought of returning to education where I knew preschoolers liked me. I even contemplated returning to teaching junior high students, even though I had vowed that I would never do that again! In the end I got into the hot tub to cry and talk to God.

My tears were a combination of pain and intercession. My heart was feeling the reality of embracing wounded people and experiencing their displaced anger. My heart was also crying out for the answer for victims of abuse. The Father compassionately replaced my broken heart with peace and my confusion with direction.

The Father asked me if I chose to forgive them. My answer was yes. He asked me if I would let go of all of the offenses that I had toward them. As I was releasing the offenses to the Father I was reminded that many times He asks me to let go of being right. You probably know how hard it is to let go of offenses when you have not done anything wrong. In these instances, I chose to forgive because I know that Jesus forgives me every time I mess up.

The Father replaced my sadness with peace. As I continued to cry out for understanding in this situation, He asked me a question that I had not expected to hear: Would I continue in the same ministry? I did not think I could be hearing God correctly because it seemed as though He was asking me to do something that I was failing in.

The Father made it clear that He disagreed with my personal assessment. He affirmed that I was doing what He wanted me to do. He reminded me that I should not be attached to the outcome of embracing broken people: My hope should be in Him, not the people that I try to help. He asked me if I would continue to love "risky" people and continue to live life with them. I said yes.

I realize that I may have to bear the consequences of irrational behavior when I invite survivors into community life. I know, however, that it is the heart of God that we provide a safe place where people can grow closer to Him while He heals their wounds.

What a Healing Community Looks Like

A healthy community is composed of people who understand brokenness and are equipped to help resolve it. These people are not intimidated by each other's issues or behaviors. They are committed to the process of renewing minds. They actually live with an understanding of Romans 12:2 for themselves as well as others: "And do not be conformed to this world, but be transformed by the renewing of your mind, so that you may prove what the will of God is, that which is good and acceptable and perfect."

A healthy community has several individuals who serve as mature spiritual leaders. We call them the spiritual mothers and fathers or, for some, spiritual grandfathers and grandmothers. Healthy communities encourage older people who are mature in faith to instruct younger people (see Titus 2).

Communities serve the needs of survivors best when they embrace them unconditionally and make them feel welcomed and honored. A successful community represents the Father's heart toward the poor in spirit by finding ways for them to belong. Acceptance is a human need that is intensified for those who have been deceived and manipulated by abuse. When community serves as a support group for those who have never been accepted, we are contributing to their healing. When we edify the person who feels disqualified, we are extending the love of God. In Ephesians 3:14–19 Paul writes:

> For this reason I bow my knees before the Father, from whom every family in heaven and on earth derives its name, that He would grant you, according to the riches of His glory, to be strengthened with power through His Spirit in the inner man, so that Christ may dwell in your hearts through faith; and that you, being rooted and grounded in love, may be able to comprehend with all the saints what is the breadth and length and height and depth, and to know the love of Christ which surpasses knowledge, that you may be filled up to all the fullness of God.

Because abuse confuses people about who they are and where they belong, they are unsure of what they have to offer to anyone else. They do not know their place within a community. They often want to contribute, but their talents have been buried for many years.

A healing community is committed to helping people discover how they can serve, and then releasing them to do so. In a small group meeting, for instance, the leader might open a discussion on spiritual gifts or offer a prayer that invites the Holy Spirit to connect those attending with the desires of their hearts. A healthy community loves the brokenhearted and desires to lead them to freedom.

Healthy spiritual communities are not threatened by the gifts that surface in survivors as they become whole. Many survivors have misused their spiritual gifts, which can lead to the conclusion that they should not be permitted to be part of the ministries within the community. Kris, for example, had a strong prophetic gift and could sense what a person was feeling. I was with her many times in church when she sensed the feelings of others, who confirmed her discernment. Kris did not understand her spiritual gift, though, and offended others by telling them what she thought their emotional state indicated. She might say, for instance, that someone was depressed because he did not understand God the way she did. This looked like arrogance, but she was really just confused about her spiritual insight and how to use it to encourage others.

I had the opportunity to watch Kris mature in her spiritual gifting. She listened to every teaching I suggested. She attended every class or home group that our church or other churches offered on spiritual gifts. She learned that her spiritual insights were intended to encourage people to move closer in their relationship with Jesus, not to give them instructions on what to do. As she learned to use her discernment, her eyes shifted from herself to the Father. If she sensed depression in someone, for instance, she would pray silently that God would bless that person with joy.

Kris is now in full-time inner healing ministry. She tells me that she is thankful that she had a community that embraced her and did not give up on her before she was healed.

The most important characteristic of a healthy community is that it focuses on the Father and strives to represent His character to those who are confused about Him. We have seen how abuse distorts the view of the Father, Jesus and the Holy Spirit. Traumatized people are often confused about where God and Christians fit into their lives of pain and sorrow. You can perhaps see that it is vitally important for the Church to extend grace to those who think that God is "bad" and responsible for their pain.

A healthy community does not operate by the standards of the world. Our spiritual home groups should not duplicate worldly recovery programs that teach survivors to try harder, stay away from bad things or disregard their pain if they have decided to follow Jesus. A community that reflects the character of the Father extends His love and kindness to the weakness of brokenhearted people. Kingdom communities should accept survivors before, during and after their scars are healed.

It is easier to embrace people when they know how to act; it is the heart of God to embrace them when they bite. We should love others because God loves us (see 1 John 4:19). Spiritual communities that love God should be committed to loving others: "Beloved, let us love one another, for love is from God; and everyone who loves is born of God and knows God" (1 John 4:7, 11).

A Survivor's View of Community

Two years ago I conducted an informal survey and asked several abuse survivors to describe their vision of a Kingdom community. I wanted to know how their connections with Christians in groups or otherwise had met their needs before, during or after healing. I included a few people who had separated from me on negative terms and who agreed to give feedback. This casual questionnaire was very insightful. Everyone who answered the survey said that "acceptance" was his or her most important need. They all wanted to feel that they were welcomed into community life unconditionally. I want to share one person's story of the healing that she received in this regard.

Liz is what many prayer ministers would call a success story. She is free from the control and domination of the evil perpetrators who began deceiving her from the time she was born. The truth has healed her mind and made her whole. She has severed all ties with her abusers by forgiving them. She is growing in the truth about God.

I asked Liz if, during the course of her healing journey, she had ever felt accepted by a spiritual community. She told me, "I believed for a long time that acceptance meant that others had to know all of the details of my life. For me that meant that they had to know that I was a satanic ritual abuse survivor with many deep, dark secrets. I have learned that what happened to me in the past doesn't have to identify my present. I have learned that acceptance has a lot to do with me knowing who I am and owning my own issues."

Liz explained that when she initially attempted to attend a spiritual small group, she was in the middle of trying to figure out who she was. She said that she expected people to understand her need to express specific details. When they did not, it felt to her like a double bind that she could not escape: She wanted to share the details of her abuse to gain their full acceptance, but she believed that if she did share the details of her abuse, no one would accept her. Revealing your secrets is scary when you are not confident in your identity. Liz confessed, "I was afraid to talk because I thought I would be rejected if I said the wrong thing."

Liz explained further, "I have learned that true acceptance comes in just being who I am in the present and not trying to guess how people will react to me. Ideally I want people who will accept all of me, but I am willing to count the cost and be myself." Liz said she now believes that a person's story of severe abuse does not need to mark a person. "Not everyone can comprehend the evil that accompanies this type of abuse," she said. "Ritual abuse is surreal to many people—they think it is too evil to be possible."

I asked Liz what specific aspect of being in a spiritual community helped her the most. She answered quickly, "Acceptance and unconditional love! I needed a place that guided me in hearing what God's truths are for me. I did not need people telling me what truth they thought I needed. I needed a place that was 'Jesus with skin.' I needed direction to discover for myself where my place in the church is."

Liz wanted to share a specific example about a spiritual community. She told me, "I started going to a church in a new city where I attended graduate school. I was still processing abuse memories. I didn't know the truth about my entire story. It was still very confusing to me, so I am sure that it sounded confusing when I tried to tell others. This church was caught up in hearing people's stories so that they could determine if the person had really given her heart to Jesus."

Liz soon found that it was very hard to serve in the church. She felt that this spiritual community was damaging to her because she had to prove herself if she wanted to serve in any capacity. They questioned her salvation; they questioned her sincerity in wanting to help in the church; they even questioned her abuse. They spoke words of such doubt and confusion that when she left that community, she was feeling demonized.

The members of that community believed that bad things do not happen to Christians. Since Liz had a rocky, traumatic past, they questioned her position in Christ. This sent Liz on a quest to become perfect and disprove what they said to her. I agree with her when she says, "Bad things happen to good Christian people!"

I asked Liz if she believed that the inner healing process of Jesus telling her the truth is the answer to healing the scars of abuse. "Yes, very much so. The hard part is learning how to walk out the healing."

Liz added that accountability is important in the healing process, but she believes it to be second to waiting patiently while God helps a survivor figure things out. Satanic ritual abuse is executed and reinforced with manipulation, domination, control and deception. Liz needed people to extend grace to her and allow her to find out some things about her journey on her own. Liz told me that after integration, it was important to her to explore her likes and dislikes apart from another person's control.

Liz wanted me to know how damaging it is for an abuse survivor to enter a spiritual community that believes the answer to healing is a program. Several churches that she attended wanted her to complete inventories to reveal to them what work she needed to do in her Christian life. Liz knows that the Holy Spirit will guide her healing journey. "I was looking for love and fellowship, not to fill my calendar with activities," Liz said.

I asked Liz to summarize her vision of an ideal spiritual community. "When you spent three days of intense inner healing ministry with me, I felt as though I had time to work through what I needed to." Liz said that an ideal community is a safe place where she can process her pain without feeling controlled. It is a place where she has the freedom to express her anger toward God. Survivors often displace their anger toward their abusers to the Father. Liz reminded me how this makes people uncomfortable, and they usually reprimand a person who is mad at God instead of understanding the nature of displaced anger.

"An ideal community is a place that has authentic worship by authentic people. Teaching is based on Scripture. It is a place where I am free to be me and figure out what my spiritual gifts are." Liz said that she had been corrected many times for choosing to stay seated during times of worship; those communities suggested, rather, that she stand or raise her hands.

I ended my survey with a question about relationship with God. I asked Liz if she feels that she is able to engage in an intimate relationship with the Father. "This is a continual struggle for me. I am better than I used to be, but it is difficult for me to believe that I do not have to perform for God to love me." Liz continued, "When I hear that God wants to bless me, it falls on deaf ears. I never know what I have to do to make God happy or to make Him listen to me. Unconditional love makes no sense to me."

Liz's honest answers revealed how abuse survivors have been told many lies about the character of our heavenly Father. Most of them believe that they have to earn His love. They want to love God, but they do not know how to be who they are and receive His love.

A healthy spiritual community knows how to welcome hurting people, love them, accept where they are in their healing journeys and lead them to Jesus, where they can experience the truth about the Father. It extends the unconditional love of God.

11

Cultivating Intimacy

D o you have a best friend who loves you unconditionally? We all desire to have relationships that are built on truth. We all want to have people in our lives who know our unresolved issues and flaws and still love us. Everyone craves intimacy. Intimacy with others and with the heavenly Father is the goal for those who desire to be like Jesus.

Fifteen years ago Ray and I met our best friends, Barbie and Don. Don introduced us to the principles of inner healing. The foundation of our relationship was centered on Jesus and our desire to be more like Him. We spent many hours every week praying together and inviting the Holy Spirit to tell us the truths about our unresolved issues. Weeks turned into months and months turned into years as our relationship transitioned into a deep friendship. We knew the truth about each other. The negative things we knew about each other did not matter because we cherished the intimacy that the four of us shared. Intimacy toward each other and intimacy with Jesus bound our hearts together.

Our fellowship was not limited to inner healing ministry. We had fun together. We traveled together. We celebrated together. We laughed a lot. We discussed our future and planned to grow old together. The years we experienced with Barbie and Don taught us the importance of deep friendships.

When ministry opportunities led Don and Barbie to relocate to another state, our close physical contact ended. Our feelings toward each other did not change, but because we no longer spent time together our relationship was different. There is a connection between intimacy and time spent together—whether that time is spent with other people or with God. Our spiritual communities should be a place where people can cultivate friendships with each other and friendship with God.

It is very important that we teach abuse survivors the importance of fellowship and friendship. A survivor who is ready to develop a close relationship with the Father will find that friendship with God is a choice and friendship with others is a choice. It is a choice that positions a person to become a joyful person:

> What we have seen and heard we proclaim to you also, that you also may have fellowship with us; and indeed our fellowship is with the Father, and with His Son Jesus Christ. These things we write, so that our joy may be made complete.
>
> 1 John 1:3–4

In the last chapter Liz explained her struggle to experience a close relationship with the Father. This is the plight of many survivors. Their history of abuse leads to wrong conclusions about having to perform to earn God's love. They repeatedly equate their heavenly Father with abusive earthly fathers who were hated and feared.

While we need to tell survivors the truth that God is good, we also should remember that experiences always overpower beliefs. We need to lead people to the presence of God so they can experience His goodness. When a traumatized person experiences the truth about God, it will change his mind about Him. Romans 2:4 says, "Do you think lightly of the riches of His kindness and tolerance and patience, not knowing that the kindness of God leads you to repentance?"

I suggest that people give God a chance. I tell them that God is not offended if they want to invite Him into new places in their hearts and see what happens. Scripture says, "O taste and see that the LORD is good; how blessed is the man who takes refuge in Him!" (Psalm 34:8). When we direct wounded hearts to the Father, He will show them His goodness.

Getting Closer to Jesus

When I talk with people about making the choice to cultivate friendship with the Father, they always ask me how to get started. By the time a person's mind has been integrated, he or she is familiar with the principle of a new mindset. I tell survivors that it is time to learn about the mindset that will enable them to experience the presence of God.

I begin by explaining that a thankful heart allows us to enter His presence (see Psalm 100:4). An appropriate mindset is focused on the good things that are connected to the Father. When people make the choice to think about truth and things that are good, they are developing a mindset that is focused on God. All good things come from the Father. A renewed mind acknowledges that God is good and chooses to live by this truth:

> Brethren, whatever is true, whatever is honorable, whatever is right, whatever is pure, whatever is lovely, whatever is of good repute, if there is any excellence and if anything worthy of praise, dwell on these things.
>
> Philippians 4:8

Jesus developed friendships, and He wants to be friends with us. This falls on deaf ears to a person who has lived an isolated life. It also does not make sense to a survivor who does not have social skills. Since it helps to give an example from Scripture, I tell them about the apostle John and Mary, the sister of Lazarus, and their friendship with Jesus. It is helpful to know that people in the Bible displayed practical signs of friendships.

I am not going to hug or rest my head on the shoulders of people that I am not in relationship with. John rested his head on Jesus' chest, displaying a sign of a comfortable friendship (see John 13:23). Mary sat at Jesus' feet to listen to Him talk (see Luke 10:39). Mary made a choice that Jesus affirmed. When my close friends are talking, I want to hear what they have to say without distractions. I want to look at them and listen. I like it when they do the same for me. Broken people lack the ability and the incentive to listen to others when they talk. This means that they often lack the incentive to listen to Jesus when He talks to them.

A Vineyard Example

In my community, when I refer to a vineyard I have to clarify whether I am referring to the Vineyard church or to actual grapevines. This is because my husband was the founding pastor of the Vineyard fellowship that our son-in-law currently pastors, and, in addition, my husband and all of our sons-in-law grow grapes. We relate well to Jesus' use of viticultural analogies. "I am the vine," He said, "you are the branches; he who abides in Me and I in him, he bears much fruit, for apart from Me you can do nothing" (John 15:5).

A large percentage of our time in the vineyards every season is spent pruning our grapes. The vine is the source from which the branches produce abundant fruit. Every vineyard worker is instructed that the vine must be the foundational source of structure and nutrition.

When we prune branches, I am always amazed that many of the branches that look good to me are cut off. They are green and healthy, but if they are turning in any direction that will hinder their ability to bear fruit, we remove them. We cannot rely on the appearance of the branches; we must operate from a deeper understanding of the goal of producing fruit. We know that producing large quantities of quality grapes is a process. We know the importance of the vine.

Jesus says that He is the vine and we are the branches. An intimate relationship with the Father includes the willingness to trust His leading in our lives. A surrendered heart has confidence in God's goodness and His desire to transform our hearts.

When we are in an intimate relationship with Jesus, we trust Him. We invite Him to prune the things in our lives that hinder our growth. We are comfortable with the fact that our transformation is a process. We are focused on the fruit of becoming more like Jesus. We have confidence that we can become like God: "You shall be Holy, for I Am Holy" (1 Peter 1:16).

Growing Friendships

When we are teaching abuse survivors the importance of developing a close relationship with the Father, we should begin by telling them about friendships with other people. It is challenging for people to value friendships if they have never had them. I like people. I like developing friendships. I like friendships that are not one-sided. Survivors, however, are often threatened when friendships begin to develop.

I prayed with Leigh for several years. God did much healing in her mind regarding the effects of her abuse. She was becoming happy. She attended church and was learning to enjoy small groups. She was expressive during worship, and told me that she felt connected to the Father when she worshiped. In her hunger for God, she spent many hours reading her Bible and Christian books. Though there were still challenges in communicating with Leigh, she was becoming easier to like. We spent time together socially, and began developing a friendship.

Yet even though Leigh and I spent many hours together, our relationship did not grow. It was off balance. I always had to initiate our visits. I always called her. When we shared a meal, I always did the cooking. Our time together was centered on Leigh and her life with no consideration for me.

Leigh was self-centered, and our conversations always came back to the topic of her abuse. She seemed obsessed with her need to find out specific details about her experience.

One day during a break in Leigh's talking, I told her of my concern for her and her unhealthy introspection. After that comment, I did not hear from her for many months. When she finally agreed to meet with me, she told me how angry she was with me. She said that she was offended that I did not agree with her fascination with her past.

I asked for her forgiveness for hurting her and tried to explain that close friendships are not threatened by differences of opinions. I wanted her to understand that solid relationships can continue to grow even when both people have opposite opinions or even opposite worldviews. Leigh did not agree. She chose her personal needs over friendship.

The parallel between an abused person's ability to develop friendships with other people and his or her ability to develop a friendship with Jesus is undeniable. The same beliefs and behaviors that hinder friendships often affect the person's beliefs and interaction with God. They usually do not trust people, and they usually do not trust God.

Traumatized people need to learn to trust others, and they need to learn to trust the Father. This can be a long and frustrating process because survivors have experienced violation by people they should have been able to trust. God is patient with them so we need to be patient with them, too (see 2 Peter 3:9).

It takes time for a hurting person to realize that she can trust. I was willing to continue investing the time to build a relationship with Leigh even though we disagreed. She believed that she could not trust me if I did not agree with her.

Liz, on the other hand, was willing to learn a new way of relating to people. She is still struggling to comprehend what it means to have a heavenly Father who is good and trustworthy. She had forty-plus years of lies about the Father; she has had only a few years with an integrated mind that desires to know the truth about God. When disappointment arises in her life, she fights not to default to the old tapes in her mind that say, "God isn't good because He didn't stop my abuse."

When Liz is in crisis, she calls me. I always begin by encouraging her that she can trust God for the answer to her problem. I suggest that she slow things down in her mind and tell me what her priority is. I always pray that she will know that she can trust God with her problems. She is learning to wait on Him because He is good and He answers her. As she looks over the many challenges she has faced in this past year, she tells me that she can reflect on His direction in every one.

Mutuality

Have you ever been in a one-sided relationship? If you want to have lunch or watch a movie with the person, you have to make the arrangements. In order for your friend to know the details of your life and vice versa, you have to coordinate coffee and conversation. One-sided relationships get old.

We can help survivors see that just as this kind of relationship with another person is fruitless, so is a narcissistic relationship with the Father fruitless. The Father does not *need* our devotion, He *wants* our devotion. God desires close fellowship with us. He wants us to talk to Him, as well as listen to Him. He does not enjoy a one-sided relationship full of demands any more than we do. Although our heavenly Father cares about supplying our needs and desires, He is worthy of praise.

Survivors can learn the importance of a thankful heart. When I am encouraging survivors to trust the Father, I suggest that when they pray they tell God that they choose Him. I help them see that they can develop a thankful heart by telling God what they appreciate about Him and what they are genuinely thankful for. Because survivors have experienced so much manipulation, they will not tell God they are thankful for something if they do not mean it because it feels manipulative to them. This is an honest answer and opens the way for us to stress sincerity in praising God.

We can suggest that they thank God for healing their minds and changing their lives. They can thank God for telling them the truth about so many aspects of their abuse. They can thank God for Jesus and the fact that He makes our healing possible.

During the inner healing process, whenever survivors receive truth in a place where they have been in bondage to a lie, I suggest that they thank God for the truth and all that it means to them. The way this is vocalized varies from person to person. Some are thankful to be separated from abuse and some are thankful for the opportunity to become more like Jesus. However they express it, this is an opportunity to implement thankfulness and develop trust in the Father. Most trauma survivors find it difficult to embrace their pasts with thankfulness. With time, however, they can embrace the truth that God can use the pain from their past for good. "And we know that God causes all things to work together for good to those who love God, to those that are called according to His purpose" (Romans 8:28).

People have told me that it helps to begin to develop a thankful heart by expressing gratitude that Jesus paid the price for their transformation. Small steps of thankfulness are appropriate when a person is overcoming a lifetime of being tricked and violated. I ask the person specifically, "What do you want your relationship with the Father to look like?" Asking the person to identify his desire for relationship with the Father is a practical way of releasing him to new levels of trust.

This question is an effective tool. I use it at the beginning of ministry sessions to activate the person's choice. I also ask this question after the person's mind has been integrated to encourage him to identify his willingness to pursue closeness with God.

Dreams for the Future

I remember when my husband and I were newlyweds receiving a modest pastor's salary, living in the church parsonage of a conservative denomination. We felt restraints on our ability to move beyond the vision of the church leadership. We were not in a position to explore options of owning our own home or generating additional income that would outpace our expected lifestyle as a pastor's household. We had a vision for our future that was not in sync with our situation. Thus, we outlined the desires of our hearts. Our dreams could only become realities if the Lord intervened. Somehow we expected them to come true.

Although our circumstances bound us to a parsonage, we drew house plans and expected a change in the direction of ministry that we could not identify. We talked about our dreams often as if they were in process. We were in a traditional denomination that had midweek services at the church but did not have small groups. Ray and I designed a house that would accommodate a house church without having a grid for how a house church works. We talked about wanting our home to be a place where people could come for emotional and physical healing. This was not common language or thought for our denomination.

I know that when Ray and I identified our dreams for our future we activated something spiritual. When we expressed faith that our dreams were possible with God, our words combined with our desires, and the Father gave us the desires of our heart (see Psalm 37:4). We knew what some of our desires were, but we did not know that they were pointing in the direction of a new ministry and new way of life for us.

In 1997 Ray and I built the house that we drew when we lived in that church parsonage. We host many Vineyard home groups in our home, as well as inner healing retreats. People who stay in our home often receive emotional healing from the scars of abuse as we minister inner healing prayer. My husband is no longer a preacher, but he is definitely a pastor. Our ministry has changed directions. Inner healing prayer ministry is a natural part of every area of our lives. We are experiencing the fruit of identifying what we wanted our life with God to look like.

Cultivating a heart that trusts the Father intimately begins with a choice to turn to Him for truth. We can help the brokenhearted learn that friendship with the Father is birthed out of confidence that He can heal the deepest scars of abuse. Intimacy grows when we learn how to be friends with Jesus. Learning to be thankful and turning to Him first are important steps. Trusting that Jesus will always tell the truth and choosing to obey His truths are significant parts of being His friend (see John 15:14).

Jesus said, "I have called you friends, for all things that I have heard from My Father I have made known to you" (John 15:15). When people realize that Jesus considers them to be His friends and that He will tell them what He hears from the Father, they are positioned to become close friends with Jesus. They are in a position to develop an intimate relationship with God because they know they can trust Him to take care of them.

"The Father helps them and delivers them; He delivers them from the wicked and saves them, because they take refuge in Him" (Psalm 37:40). May this be our theme as we reach out to the brokenhearted.

12

Top Ten Keys
for Overcoming Trauma

There are no set patterns to follow in inner healing ministry, as it is outlined in this book, precisely because we ask the Holy Spirit to speak as He will to the hearts and minds of those who have come to us for help. Nevertheless, when working with survivors of childhood abuse or incest, or anyone who has experienced wounding, certain factors seem to facilitate the journey to the Father's heart. Here, then, are ten keys you might share with someone who wants to open the door to healing and wholeness.

1. Choose to live in truth.

"You will know the truth and the truth will make you free."

John 8:32

In order to walk in freedom, a wounded individual must make a commitment to truth no matter how scary the truth might seem. It means asking the Father, through the ministry of the Holy Spirit, to reveal painful memories.

The initial part of this process is hearing the Father's word on the issue. To stop at that point, however, is to stop short of freedom. Next comes the commitment to receive and believe the truth. Understanding that God will shine a light on the truth will help survivors begin the healing process. We need to encourage them to invite the Father to tell them the truth about their abuse.

2. Choose to give God permission to search your heart.

Search me, O God, and know my heart; try me and know
my anxious thoughts.

Psalm 139:23

This may be the most vital step in the transformation process: choosing to stop denying the painful things that are
hidden in the mind. Denial happens when some truth is
too hard to accept. It is a method of hiding unresolved
memories that one cannot make sense of.

Even when survivors desire to know the truth, their
strong defense mechanisms can block them from doing
so. People with fractured souls need help understanding
that if they were capable of processing on their own what
they are denying, they would have figured it out by now. In
fact, if they try to figure out what is hidden, their protective
and defensive thoughts will interfere. They need help to
see that the Holy Spirit is the only one capable of showing
them what they are denying, when they began denying it
and the reason they are denying it.

As they submit to the Holy Spirit, He will search out
whatever is important for them to know. Jesus is the one
who knows the hearts of all (see Acts 1:24). Understanding the role of the Holy Spirit in breaking through denial
is a key that will open to remembrance places that were
once forbidden.

3. Choose to forgive, forgive, forgive and keep on forgiving.

"Forgive us our debts, as we also have forgiven our debtors."

Matthew 6:12

Trauma survivors often resist the process of forgiveness, because to them forgiving their perpetrators means agreeing with the abuse. We must teach survivors to choose to forgive other people because Jesus forgives us. Ephesians 4:32 says, "Be kind to one another, tender-hearted, forgiving each other, just as God in Christ also has forgiven you." This is the way to a clean heart (see Psalm 51:10) and becoming more like Jesus. If they are willing to forgive others, they will have greater understanding of grace and truth. The Father is grace and truth, and the Father forgives people who do not deserve it.

We are able to forgive other people because God forgives us. Understanding the truth about the power of forgiveness is an important key to healing a heart that was hardened by the scars of abuse.

4. Choose not to remain offended.

"But I say to you, love your enemies and pray for those who persecute you."

Matthew 5:44

Freedom cannot be experienced by those who remain in a state of offence toward those who abused them. Although unforgiveness and holding offenses are closely related, it is easier for a person who has been violated to forgive his or her perpetrators than it is to let go of the things he or she wants to hold against them.

When victims are willing to forgive their abusers but still want to seek revenge, they are still offended. They must take the next step and be willing to let go of every aspect of the violation that gives them a "right" to remain angry. When they can pray sincerely for those who abused them, they have let go of their offenses. When they can ask God to heal and restore their perpetrators, they are forgiving others the way God forgives them (see Colossians 3:13).

God is the only one who has the right to deal with people's sins (see Romans 12:19). We need to encourage trust in God to deal with injustice in His time and in His manner. We can concur that forgiving abusive people and letting go of offenses toward them is not a natural response, but that God will help them. That is God's way. Letting go of grievances and choosing not to be offended is an important key to healing.

5. Choose to accept your true identity.

> But you are a chosen race, a royal priesthood, a holy nation, a people for God's own possession, so that you may proclaim the excellencies of Him who has called you out of darkness into His marvelous light.
>
> 1 Peter 2:9

Traumatized people have believed many lies about themselves. When they allow others to define them, they are separated from the truth about who God says they are. Someone who is confused about his identity often creates a false self to present to the world.

We can ask individuals receiving ministry to tell us how they came to have such negative conclusions about themselves. Sometimes in answering this question, they discover their own faulty thinking and even recognize some lies they have believed.

No one can be healed and made whole by allowing the lies of the past to determine his identity. He will not know what he likes or does not like. He will have forgotten or never known his gifts and talents.

Survivors are usually surprised to learn that 1 Peter 2:9 calls us royalty. Healing and transformation must include giving God permission to tell them the truth about who He says they are. They need to see that their identity is connected to God. They are holy because He is holy (see 1 Peter 1:16).

6. Choose to connect with the desires of your heart.

Delight yourself in the LORD; and He will give you the desires of your heart.

Psalm 37:4

Trauma victims are often disconnected from positive emotions—which fuel desires and passions. It is much easier for them to relate to negative emotions. Yet it is the positive feelings that allow people to move forward and make their dreams come true.

The effects of abuse restrict people from believing that it is okay to receive the good things that the Father wants them to have. As Matthew 7:11 says, "How much more will your Father who is in heaven give what is good to those who ask Him!" Survivors often say that they do not believe they can ask God to heal them and give them what they long for. They feel unworthy even to ask Him for good things. They think that He does not care about the desires of their hearts.

Sometimes we have to help trauma victims find an explanation for their lack of passion. They usually say that they could move forward if they truly believed that God wanted them to have good things. At this point we can suggest that they give themselves and God permission to release the desires of their hearts. This is a very useful key for those who are trapped in lies about their dreams.

7. Choose to ask Jesus for help.

"And whatever things you ask in prayer believing, you will receive."

Matthew 21:22

"What do you want Jesus to do for you?" Abuse survivors have trouble admitting that they need help, because the adults who should have protected them as they navigated childhood were abusing them. This leads to an unhealthy, independent attitude that no one can help them. We can assure desperate people not only that Jesus is able to help them, but that He wants to help them.

Asking Jesus for help is simple; we need only to know what we want Him to do for us. Wounded people rarely know what to ask Jesus for. They feel disqualified and undeserving of healing and freedom. They are disconnected from the idea that the Father wants to give them good things. They find it hard to believe that healing their scars of abuse begins by asking Jesus to help them.

Jesus says that if we believe that He can help us and we ask Him to help us, He will. We can encourage people to begin by asking Jesus to help them with one thing at a time until their experience matches their request. When survivors become confident that Jesus will help them in small things, they are comfortable asking Him to heal deeper things. This develops trust and strengthens a friendship with Jesus.

8. Choose to reassess the supernatural workings of the Holy Spirit.

"But when He, the Spirit of truth, comes, He will guide you into all the truth."

John 16:13

The Holy Spirit works in supernatural ways. He reveals the truth about a painful past and also lights the way to freedom. The Holy Spirit did this in the New Testament Church, and He is still doing it today.

Survivors are skeptical about this because they believe many lies about the supernatural. Those who experienced demonic presence during times of abuse usually define the supernatural realm by those evil experiences. Plus, many children being abused are told that if God were powerful He would rescue them. Since the evil continues to hurt them, they conclude that Satan is more powerful than God. Thus, they are usually afraid of anything related to the spirit realm because it seems to signify demonic activity and the devil's power. This makes them afraid of the Father's supernatural character and resistant to the ministry of Jesus and the Holy Spirit.

We can help them understand the truth about God's power and the work of the Holy Spirit. When they invite Him to direct their lives, they are positioning themselves to experience the truth about the supernatural and remove blocks to healing.

9. Choose to engage in Kingdom community.

For the body is not one member, but many.

1 Corinthians 12:14

An important key to overcoming the scars of abuse is connecting to healthy people who share Kingdom values. Being connected to a Christian community means that we joyfully share resources, preferences, needs, risks, values and beliefs with others who do the same and are committed to loving us and God. Our true identities are revealed in such a group.

Our Father has designed Kingdom community as a place where we can become the fullness of all He intends us to be. It is designed to be a place where we are safe to explore who we are, where every individual can uncover what the Father has deposited in him or her. Spiritual gifts can be discerned, understood, refined and released. Community is a place where others can help us with our healing journeys.

This is principally because a Kingdom community is a place where people are focused on God. It is here that we learn the details about the Father and how to become like Him. God compares Kingdom community to the human body and its optimum ability to function in health—when each part within the system is healthy and contributing to the overall operation (see 1 Corinthians 12).

Trauma survivors are often afraid to enter a spiritual community because they think it is safer to live a solitary life. This lie keeps them from knowing who God is. We need to help people realize that wholeness cannot occur outside of a healthy godly community.

10. Choose to commit to a lifestyle of intimacy with Father God.

We love, because He first loved us.

1 John 4:19

People who come for ministry need to think about what they want their lives with God to look like. It helps for them to write their thoughts down. The next step is to be honest about what they are willing to do to develop the relationship they want to have with Him.

If they understand the importance of developing close friendships in their communities, they can see an important parallel: Becoming a friend with Jesus leads to friendship with the Father. Survivors learn to hear the voice of God by listening to Jesus, because Jesus says and does what the heavenly Father shows Him (see John 5:19).

There are many things they can do to enhance their love for and devotion to God: spending time meditating on His Word and telling Him what they appreciate about Him and what they are thankful for, for example. Thanksgiving should be specific and focus on God's goodness to them. This can also be a time of prayer or a time of singing or dancing. They can start with a small amount of time initially so that they will desire time with God and not feel obligated. Learning to love God as He loves us is an important key to intimate friendship with Him.

In Closing

Here is my prayer for you as you minister the love of Jesus to those with fractured souls:

[May] Christ . . . dwell in your [heart] through faith; and that you, being rooted and grounded in love, may be able to comprehend with all the saints what is the breadth and length and height and depth, and to know the love of Christ which surpasses knowledge, that you may be filled up to all the fullness of God.

Ephesians 3:17–19

Index

Candyce Roberts lives in Campbellsville, Kentucky, with her husband, Ray, where they share life with their three daughters, sons-in-law and ten grandchildren. She enjoys living in the country and having her family as neighbors. Over the river and through the woods really does apply to visits from her grandchildren.

Candyce, who has worked in full-time inner healing ministry with abuse survivors for fifteen years, has an effective manner in leading the brokenhearted to Jesus for healing. She has genuine compassion for those trapped in the pain of abuse and desires to help their fractured souls find healing and deliverance.

Many abuse survivors, in fact, move to Campbellsville to receive focused inner healing ministry because of the success she has leading fractured people to freedom. With a focus on finding God's truth, her holistic approach to healing includes developing a life with Jesus and others while receiving inner healing ministry.

Candyce has a vision for a safe house facility where abuse survivors can live while receiving inner healing ministry. The house would be a transition place for abuse survivors who need healing and deliverance from the scars of their past while learning truths about God and themselves.

On a lighter note, Candyce is a closet artist who hopes one day to produce beautiful works that others cannot live without.